To Gary & Sawyer

Baseball forever

Dorothy Kirby Hull

Dizzy

DEAN OF BASEBALL & MY PODNAH

By

Gene Kirby

With Bo Carter & Mark S. McDonald

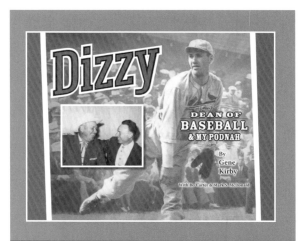

International Standard Book Number (ISBN): 978-0-9909711-3-9

First printing

Graphics design created by Dust Devil Books, Midland, Texas, published by Cool Cat Communications.

Published by Cool Cat Communications
P.O. Box 701713
San Antonio, TX 78270

To order more copies of this book, please visit www.sportsandoutdoors.guru.
Or, email coolcatcomm@att.net.

About the Cover

In the mid-1930s, with the U.S. in the throes of the Great Depression, Dizzy Dean gave America a chance to laugh. Before an eager audience dressed in neckties and period straw hats, Dizzy loosens up before a St. Louis Cardinals spring training game in Florida. When the pitcher retired, his popularity only grew, thanks to national TV exposure of CBS Game of the Week. Producer for Dean, Gene Kirby wrote many of the tales in this manuscript and collected the old images.

Dedication

To my son, Glenn,
in grateful appreciation for his meaningful
contribution to this book ... and to my life.

Editor's Note

Much of this original manuscript was produced by Dizzy Dean's longtime friend, Gene Kirby, who also served as the pitcher's broadcasting colleague and confidant. Dean's play-by-play man Pee Wee Reese took one last fond look back at Dizzy, while Kirby's late son, Glenn, wrote the moving and analytical epilogue. Project coordinator Bo Carter and editor Mark S. McDonald also contributed passages. The varied authors are noted with a credit line at the end of each vignette. Every effort was made to retain the writer's voice and the spirit engendered by the Dizzy Dean-Gene Kirby relationship. – *McD*

Preface

About this Book

Fifty years ago, my dad Gene Kirby, began a journey of telling the story about his *podnah*, Dizzy Dean. I was just a small girl then, but I vividly remember Dizzy as a big man with a big personality and a big hat.

Now, these impressions have been brought to life through my Dad's account about Dizzy, the man, and the life he lived. From the cotton fields of Arkansas, to the Army, to the baseball diamond, Dizzy wound up in front of the microphone with my Dad.

Dad recounted to me many stories of his time with Dizzy, Pee Wee Reese and so many others throughout his own career in sports. And while most of these tales had a firm foundation in truth, I suspect stretching that truth was probably part of the storytelling. Let's just say Dad had a way of telling a story, animated in delivery and luring you to the apex.

But the stories you will find here are not just about a baseball legend, they are about my father and his relationship with Dizzy Dean, their travels, the people they met and most certainly, the colorful banter and bull**** that transpired between them for nearly 20 years.

This book represents years of starts and stops, and adversities along the way. At one time, my brother Glenn started to help Dad finish the book and after doing an interview with Pee Wee Reese one evening, died in a car accident. It was devastating for our whole family and Dad just couldn't face completing the book.

So here we are now. Dad has since passed away and I'm taking up the mantle to bring this project to completion; bottom of the 9th, 2 men out, and batting for the home team to win (Couldn't resist the metaphor!).

As work began again, I enlisted the help of Mark McDonald and Bo Carter. Our meetings and subsequent communication through the publishing process have been filled with much emotion, nostalgia, sadness and joy. I am reminded of growing up a bit differently than others, in ballparks watching games, traveling with teams during summer vacation, moving frequently when Dad's jobs changed, like an Army brat but through baseball.

I am also reminded of Dad's great love of storytelling and having read many of Glenn's notes during his interviews for the book, what a gifted writer he was in setting the scene of Dean's life and in a more poignant way our dad's life.

Through Dad's original manuscript and editing by Mark and Bo, I hope we have done him proud. It is a story of Americana, baseball, and friendship.

Much love to my mother Dorothy, brother Kevin, sister Wendy and, especially, my husband Doug.

–Sara Kirby Burke
2016

About the Author

Gene Kirby was a veteran of many years in the field of sports broadcasting as a producer, announcer, director and writer.

A pro's pro, Gene worked with Dizzy Dean for more than 20 years. This included Dizzy's baseball broadcasts with the Mutual Radio Network's Game of the Day, then ABC and CBS Television Games of the Week. Adding to the depth of their working relationship, Gene traveled extensively with Dean through hundreds of public appearances around the country for Falstaff Brewing Corp. of St. Louis and the advertising agency, Dancer-Fitzgerald-Sample, in New York.

After the Dean era, Kirby worked in baseball with the Montreal Expos as traveling secretary and administrative assistant and director of broadcasting. He also worked with the Philadelphia Phillies as executive director for radio and television broadcasts and later served as vice president for administration and broadcasting with the Boston Red Sox.

When Hollywood came calling, Gene served as baseball consultant for the award-winning movie "The Natural," starring Robert Redford, Glenn Close and Kim Basinger.

All told, Kirby had over 50 years of experience in sports broadcasting, radio and television, along with 25-plus years in various facets of Major League Baseball. His expertise also included stints with the St. Louis Hawks as an announcer in the National Basketball Association, Army football on WINS Radio in New York, Southern Conference basketball, and producer for "Great Moments in Sports" on network radio for the U.S. Air Force.

The author also contributed stories to MLB game programs and scorecards, along with the New York Times, and national magazines such *The Sporting News, Baseball America and Sports Heritage.*

Kirby retired in 1982 to Florida, where he died in 2011. He was 95.

Table of Contents

Part I

Pre-Game Warmup

INTRODUCTION

It was a match made in baseball heaven. Just as the national pastime was riding a tsunami of popularity in the mid-1930s, a colorful right-hander from central casting – or was it Louisiana? or Texas? – burst onto America's public stage with a blazing fastball and a steaming dose of humor to match. The timing could not have been better.

Dizzy Dean was a complicated, colorful, gifted athlete who, like another bygone baseball hero, Babe Ruth, emerged from a patchy childhood into the American consciousness. Dizzy, too, had a similar homespun, "howdy, podnah" personality that connected with the great unwashed at a time in our history when common folks badly needed a chuckle.

In the lean years of the Great Depression, known as the Dirty Thirties, most Americans lived close to the edge. Jobs were hard to come by. Food and shelter were the necessities; an apple for dessert was a luxury. Set against this grim backdrop, baseball fans east

The toast of baseball after his St. Louis Cardinals won the 1934 World Series and being named Associated Press Athlete of the Year, Dizzy Dean takes an exaggerated wind-up during spring training, 1935, in Bradenton, Florida. Why not? Almost everything Dizzy did was bigger than life.

of the Mississippi, even the jobless and hungry, would find momentary relief as they gathered 'round the family's clunky, couch-sized Zenith Stratosphere for World Series radio broadcasts. Out West, fans eager for box scores and highlights had to wait until the next morning's paper.

You could buy a new Chevy for $635. Average rent was $22 a month. A loaf of bread cost 8 cents. But with one in five Americans out of work, who could afford such things?

The family doctor made $3,382 a year, often trading his medical treatment for a

Once his playing career was over, Dizzy Dean's public profile grew even larger, thanks to his antics in the broadcast booth on Game of the Week. Here, Dean and his long-time sidekick Gene Kirby, who wrote much of this book's manuscript, make ready for a 1954 game at old Connie Mack Stadium in Philadelphia.

sack of home-grown tomatoes or a mowed lawn. A public school teacher made $1,227 a year, needing odd jobs or tutoring in the summer to stay fed. A registered nurse exchanged her bedside manner and a year of countless hours on her feet for $936.

Mindless farming practices from western Nebraska and Kansas into eastern Colorado and northeastern New Mexico had turned once-fertile grasslands into the Dust Bowl. The same airborne silt smothered the panhandles of Oklahoma and Texas. The Dust Bowl, combined with tight money and labor union strikes, drove up the cost of meat, milk and produce. With food expensive – if it was available at all – fear and unrest grew rampant.

Across the pond, news was no better. Adolph Hitler was beginning to make his move, re-arming Germany, persecuting Jews and stirring suppression and fierce nationalistic pride among Germans at the expense of personal liberty.

Certainly there were advancements both here and abroad.

Walt Disney brought to the screen his first Technicolor film, nine minutes of Mickey Mouse and Donald Duck. Prohibition was lifted, shedding sunlight into the wink-wink of the backroom speakeasy while creating a market for innovations such as the first canned beer – Krueger's Cream Ale, of Richmond, Virginia. A chemist at DuPont announced a new synthetic material that came to be known as nylon, a discovery that gave rise to everything from strap-on casts for broken ankles to storm gutters to batting helmets and catcher's shin guards.

Socially and culturally, the American woman was still a long way from full equality, but the sheer weight of her numbers began to show up in election results, hiring practices and consumer spending. Solo cross-oceanic flights of Amelia Earhart and the golf of Babe Didrickson Zaharias inspired millions of young girls.

Despite progress in medicine, communication and transportation, note that period photos rarely show working-class people smiling. Instead, their cheeks are gaunt with hunger, their grim foreheads creased by missed mortgage payments, their weary eyes dull from years of stress and doubt, even hopelessness.

For a sweaty, struggling nation, baseball became more than a distraction. The grand old game was an escape. And for Dizzy Dean, in the right place with the right stuff at the right time, the pitcher's mound became a stepladder to an even bigger stage.

Never one to be ignored, "Ol' Diz," as he referred to himself, was alternately beloved and reviled. Profane, direct, clubhouse irritant and a money-grubbing check-dodger, Dizzy was forever quarreling with management over contract demands. Then again, Dizzy was generous to a fault, loyal to family and the consummate showman who had the competitive heart of a lion.

Opponents viewed him as a braggart, an unprofessional jackass who needed a lesson in manners. Rivals itching to deliver a proper fist to Dizzy's honker would have stood in a long line, behind even some of the showboat's own teammates.

More than controversial, Dizzy was combustible; a can of gasoline just waiting for a spark. Following his Hall of Fame diamond days, he mellowed a bit – not entirely – and rose to folk icon status as millions of Americans invited him into their homes every Saturday. Alongside Pee Wee Reese in the broadcast booth, Dizzy and the CBS television crew delivered "Game of the Week" telecasts produced by Gene Kirby and Falstaff Brewing Corp. By the 1950s and into the '60s, Dizzy had become better known to a larger audience for TV work and public appearances than for his exploits with the 1930s St. Louis Cardinals Gas House Gang.

Small wonder this double dose of Dizzy Dean made such an impression on Americans, and not just baseball fans. People from all walks of life – just folks – were drawn to the man who spoke his version of truth to power with the drawl of a Southern sharecropper and the

self-belief of a world-beater. Americans couldn't get enough of Dizzy Dean and the reverse was also true. Just as we needed a Dizzy figure, he seemed to flourish with the attention and withered without it.

This perfect alignment, as you will see in the pages to follow, is brought to life again by the words and images of those who knew Dizzy the best. Chief among them other than Dizzy's fiercely loyal and sometimes controlling wife Pat – a battle axe if you crossed her – was the late Gene Kirby, who worked with Dizzy on behalf of Falstaff. Lucky for us, Kirby, a former Major League Baseball announcer and front-office exec, was a steadfast keeper of memorabilia, and quite the spinner of yarns.

Dean tales and publicity shots left to Kirby were in turn left to Gene's children. Taken together, these relics remind us of Dizzy's immense popularity, but also why the flawed human of a pitcher was so beloved.

At once, you will see that for Dizzy and Kirby, their work became play. Their

play became work. From 1949 to 1965, their rollicking relationship transcended the game, spilling out of the TV booth into golf, horse racing, night clubs, private homes, speaking engagements, charity events, pranks and practical jokes.

We're lucky that a storyteller recognized the value of these moments and saved snapshots and yellowed news clips from yesteryear. Over a 38-year period, Kirby wrote down Dizzy's antics and his own thoughts, first on a manual Underwood typewriter and later on an IBM Selectric, aided by careful brush strokes of Liquid Paper.

Kirby, upon his death in 2011, left these priceless treasures to his children, who stored them in almost-forgotten cardboard boxes. The images and news accounts, a mosaic of the era, paint a detailed picture of Dizzy Dean, unvarnished and in full detail. I came to understand that Dizzy was more than a successful, blow-hard pitcher, but a product of his time. It became clear what Dizzy meant to the culture, and why his sudden passing struck America with such jarring impact.

In 1974, the year of Dean's death, a frayed nation, recovering from the complexities of race riots, government scandal and the bloody realities of Vietnam, was but a generation removed from the soft, sepia-tone mental snapshots of an unvarnished right-hander. There he was, Dizzy still standing on the mound of our minds, baseball in hand ... cocky and tall in that baggy flannel uniform ... waiting to deliver his next pitch, his next laugh.

Then as now, the legacy of Dizzy Dean has been traced in many books. You might wonder, do we really need yet another book on Billy the Kid? Or Patton? Or Custer's last stand? This one is different.

Thanks largely to insight from Gene Kirby, gained over countless days with Dizzy Dean and his friends, we are reminded how baseball was once played, but so much more. Kirby's early work gives us a glimpse of how we viewed the world, how we treated each other, how

life was lived, in a simpler place and time.

These were the days of America, of Gene Kirby and his famous running buddy, Jay Hanna Dean. May you, too, enjoy the journey. Or, as Dizzy often said, "hang onto your hat, podnah!" – *Editor, Mark S. McDonald*

Dizzy Dean, along with his wife, Pat, might have been tough in contract negotiations, but when it came to kids, he was a pushover.

In a rare 1935 photo, the Dean family gathered in Hot Springs, Arkansas, to celebrate the opening of the Dizzy Dean Baseball School. Top row, left to right, are Dizzy, brother Elmer and brother Paul, a noted pitcher for the Cardinals in his own right. Below Dizzy is his wife, Patricia, next to his father, A.M., and Paul's wife, Dorothy.

Jay Hanna Dean

Born – Jan. 16, 1910, to Albert Monroe Dean and Alma Nelson Dean in Lucas, Arkansas.

1917 – Alma Nelson Dean dies, buried near Log Cabin, Arkansas.

1920 – Family moves to Yell County, Arkansas.

1924 – Family moves to Oklahoma; attends school only sporadically.

1926 – Drops out of school for good, joins U.S. Army, assigned to Fort Sam Houston, San Antonio.

1929 – Gets tryout with St. Louis Cardinals.

1930 – After indifferent military career, signs free agent contract with St. Louis Cardinals.

1930 – Makes MLB debut with Cards, then sent to minor league affiliate in Houston.

1931 – Marries Patricia Nash, First Christian Church, Houston.

1932 – Cards recall Dizzy to St. Louis; At age 22, Dizzy is back in The Show to stay.

1934 – Posts a 30-7 win-loss record, plus another seven saves (unofficial); MVP; wins two World Series games vs. Detroit; named Associated Press athlete of the year.

1937 – Struck on the foot by an Earl Averill line drive, suffers a broken toe.

Favoring his injured foot, alters pitching motion while pitching virtually every other day, arm-weary Dizzy loses his fastball.

1941 – While with the Chicago Cubs, Dizzy retires. Begins radio-TV career, calling games for the Cards and St. Louis Browns.

1947 – At age 37, leaves the press box one last time, pitching four scoreless innings for the Browns in a sudden and final comeback.

1950-51 – Serves in radio booth for Yankees.

1952 – Works radio booth for Mutual network.

1953 – Inducted into Baseball Hall of Fame; does radio-TV for ABC.

1955-65 – In high-profile TV work, teams first with Buddy Blattner (through 1959) then becomes a broadcast legend with Pee Wee Reese (through 1965).

1966 – Does radio broadcasts of Atlanta Braves games, as CBS yields Game of the Week rights to NBC, which names Curt Gowdy as anchor voice.

Late 1960s – Moves with wife Patricia to her hometown of Bond, Mississippi.

July 17, 1974 – Dizzy Dean dies in Reno, Nevada at the age of 64

1996 – Dizzy Dean Museum opens in Jackson, Mississippi, adjacent to Mississippi Sports Hall of Fame.

STARTING AT THE END

Wednesday night, July 17, 1974, was playing out like a routine grounder to short to end the ninth in newsrooms across the country as copy jockeys on sports desks plugged in the day's final box scores and recaps of America's pastime. Massive printing presses began churning out tomorrow's editions, when suddenly, bells rang. *Ding-ding-ding.*

Wire services of the day fitted their teletypes with bells, which rang to warn a major news story was forthcoming. This was news all right: Banner headlines would announce the incomparable Dizzy Dean had just passed away.

During one of his annual visits to Reno, Nevada, the pitcher-turned-television personality died. Heart attack.

The iconic baseball player who had been cheered for providing millions of Americans with respite from the Great Depression days of the 1930s was gone. As a pitcher, he was masterful, the last 30-game winner in the National League. Later, Dean was a colorful announcer who brought smiles to the Baby Boomer generation in the 1950s and 1960s. He was memorialized in hundreds of written and photo tributes, all recounting his long and colorful career.

In a way, Jay Hanna "Dizzy" Dean's death was as newsworthy as his life. It is not often that a standing president of the United States offers condolences to the family of a sports figure. Dizzy was the exception.

"To my generation of Americans, Dizzy Dean will always be remembered as the blazing young fast-baller who led the Gashouse Gang of St. Louis to the pinnacle of baseball glory," President Richard Nixon said in a prepared statement. "To the younger generation he will be remembered as the entertaining weekly voice of baseball on national television.

"Dizzy was a true American treasure, and our sympathy goes out to the Dean family after his passing."

Dean's body was flown from Reno to New Orleans, where it was received by family members. Along the drive to Wiggins, Mississippi, fans gathered on the roadside to catch a glimpse of the passing hearse. Well-wishers and family members packed the First Baptist Church of Bond, Mississippi, July 20, 1974, to hear Rev. Bill Taylor deliver the eulogy. The church choir sang several of Dizzy's favorite classic hymns.

Football coaching legends and long-time golfing buddies and Dean broadcast fans Johnny Vaught of Ole Miss and Paul ("Bear") Bryant of Alabama helped Dizzy's widow, Pat, into the church. Afterwards, she was greeted by many of the attendees under a shade tree outside the main entrance.

Among the other mourners paying respects were several former Major League ballplayers from Alabama, Mississippi and Louisiana, along with a number of network executives.

"It was a total zoo," recalls Rick

Veteran newspaper columnist Rick Cleveland, a sports historian and executive director of the Mississippi Sports Hall of Fame, remembers vividly the shock and sorrow that greeted the sudden death of Dizzy Dean. The funeral, Cleveland says, was "a zoo."

Cleveland, longtime sports columnist and current executive director of the Mississippi Sports Hall of Fame and Dizzy Dean Museum in Jackson, Mississippi. Cleveland, then in his 20s, attended with his father Ace, former sports information director at Southern Mississippi University.

"We sat behind Bear Bryant and Johnny Vaught, and I kept thinking about all the sports figures who were there. I think the governor of Mississippi (Bill Waller, 1972-76) was there.

"When my dad saw that line of cars trying to get into the parking lot and the throng of people already outside the church, he said: 'Oh, no (in a little stronger language). When the preacher of that little church sees that crowd and the people attending, he might give his longest sermon ever.' As I recall, it lasted a long time."

The entire town of Wiggins – all businesses and commerce – closed from 10 a.m.-noon on Saturday, and mourners from as far away as Appleton, Wisconsin, paid their respects during Friday night visitation at the local funeral home.

Rev. Taylor did not expound on Dizzy's baseball career except to mention the Baseball Hall of Fame. He spoke of Pat's faith and her desire to see Diz succeed in all endeavors, and his aim to be a role model for youngsters.

Rick Cleveland said the message might have lasted 35-40 minutes, and everyone was near heat stroke in a 400-seat church with no air conditioning.

Mourners included Dizzy's younger brother, Paul, who joined Bryant and Vaught in stopping to speak to Pat Dean. They lauded Dizzy's powerful and positive impact on the American culture.

Dizzy's partner in the broadcast booth, Gene Kirby, was one of the honorary pallbearers, joining country music legend Roy Acuff, vocalist Phil Harris, Dallas car dealership owner W.O. Bankston and several other family friends.

Outside the church, an estimated 800-900 mourners listened to the service through speakers.

Newspapers across the nation chronicled the funeral and printed accolades from former teammates, opponents and sports writers. Here are some of the glowing tributes to one of the most remarkable characters of his time.

– Bo Carter

Dean family collection, courtesy of Gene Kirby

In the prime of his baseball career, this 1934 shot caught Dizzy Dean between laughs.

"When ole Diz was out there pitching it was more than just another ball game. It was a regular three-ring circus and everybody was wide awake and enjoying being alive."

– Pepper Martin, longtime Cardinals teammate

"You were attracted by the graceful rhythm of his pitching motion; the long majestic sweep of his arm as he let the ball fly; the poised alertness after the pitch. That was what counted and you knew it when batter after batter swung ineptly at pitches they couldn't even see."

– New York Times editorial

"As a ballplayer, (Dizzy) Dean was a natural phenomenon like the Grand Canyon or the Great Barrier Reef. Nobody ever taught him baseball and he never had to learn. He was just doing what came naturally when a scout named Don Curtis discovered him on a Texas sandlot and gave him his first contract."

– Pulitzer Prize-winning columnist Red Smith

"Dizzy Dean was born in Arkansas with a golden wisecrack in his mouth, ants in his pants and an abiding faith in humanity."

– J. Roy Stockton, St. Louis Post-Dispatch and The Sporting News

Legendary pitcher Dizzy Dean, crossing the plate in a yellowed and cracked print from the mid-1930s, was a gritty and colorful competitor in all facets of baseball. This made Dizzy a fan favorite, admired by all-time great Babe Ruth, who by 1935 had been traded from the Yankees to the Braves.

Dean family collection, courtesy of Gene Kirby

Part II

The Early Daze of Diz

OVERVIEW — A CHARACTER RISES FROM MODEST ROOTS

Jay Hanna ("Dizzy") Dean was born January 16, 1910, in Lucas, Arkansas, during one of those trying times in U.S. history. It was four years before hostilities broke out in Europe, and six years before the U.S. entered World War I.

These were hardscrabble times for a family of sharecroppers moving to wherever ripe cotton needed picking – Arkansas, Oklahoma, Texas and Mississippi. Electricity was non-existent in most of these rural areas, and the automobile would not gain widespread use in the country locales until after the Great War. Dizzy's parents, Albert and Alma Dean, eked out the family's existence by sharecropping. Mrs. Dean made a few coins doing odd jobs.

Jay Dean dropped out of school after the third grade to help in the cotton fields, and without an education appeared destined to a life of poverty. Enlisting in the U.S. Army provided an escape of sorts. In 1928, Dean signed on with Uncle Sam, but baseball would become his hot ticket. While on weekend

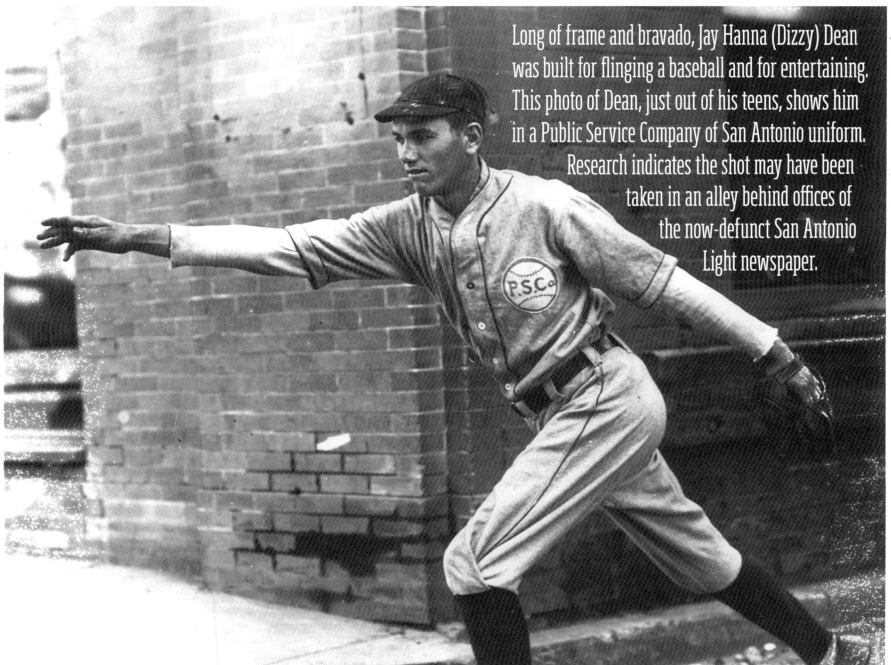

Long of frame and bravado, Jay Hanna (Dizzy) Dean was built for flinging a baseball and for entertaining. This photo of Dean, just out of his teens, shows him in a Public Service Company of San Antonio uniform. Research indicates the shot may have been taken in an alley behind offices of the now-defunct San Antonio Light newspaper.

A product of her hard times, Alma Dean died when son Jay was 7, after working beside her husband, Ab, in the fields as a sharecropper. Later, Dizzy Dean lamented the loss of his mother, when both were so young.

Dean family collection, courtesy of Gene Kirby

leave, Dean spent his free time pitching for local and semi-pro teams in the San Antonio-New Braunfels, Texas area.

Semi-pro teams in that era typically played every weekend, sometimes as many as three games, and mound aces like Dizzy might be called upon to pitch upwards of 18-20 innings as a starter or in relief during a 24-36 hour period. In the summer of 1929 the hard-throwing right-hander is said to have won 16 games for his various teams, while pitching almost solely on weekends. Before summer's end that year, Dizzy "bought" his way out of active Army duty, which was common practice under peacetime policy. Those weekend baseball outings, not his military service, caught the eye of pro scouts.

Tryouts eventually led to Dizzy signing with the St. Louis Cardinals in 1930, which launched an illustrious career climb through the minors that took him through St. Joseph, Missouri, (Class B), and Houston, Texas, (then Class AA). In these two whistle stops during 1930-31, the Cardinals farmhand posted eye-popping statistics: 51-20 in 87 games, including 64 starts.

It was a rousing start for a pitching standout seldom known for his humility – Dizzy's real bragging would start soon enough. – *Bo Carter*

THERE'S ALWAYS A BEGINNING

(BUT WITH DIZZY, WHERE AND WHEN?)

★

Alone I walked on the ocean strand,
I stooped and wrote upon the sand
My name, the year, the day.
A wave came rolling high and fast
and washed my lines away.

–Howard Gould

Contrary to some sources, his name *was* Jay Hanna Dean. Date of birth: January 16, 1910. Place: Logan County on the Ledgerwood Farm, Lucas, Arkansas.

Setting the record straight now may not be the banner headline news it might have been in the 1930s when Dizzy was at the height of his great baseball career. But it does offer admirers of the great one at long last factual reference to one birthday, one name and one birthplace just like the rest of us mortals.

This is significant because for most of his adult life, Dizzy Dean reportedly was born in three different towns and on three different dates. He was also known by two different names: Jay Hanna and Jerome Herman. Creating this confusion was Ol' Diz himself. It would have been too simple, and not as much fun, to give three sportswriters working for three different newspapers the same story. Nobody gets his name in the papers, consistently, that is, that way.

The home where the Dean family lived in the 1920s in Lucas, Arkansas, was still standing in the 1960s when this snapshot was believed to have been taken. This school in Lucas did not long contain young Jay Dean. He dropped out in the third grade.

Even if you are the greatest pitcher ever in baseball – an admission not hard to come by when listening to Dizzy Dean.

To one writer Dizzy said he was born on July 4, 1911, in Holdenville, Oklahoma. This happens to be Independence Day, and Holdenville is the town where he attended school, if ever so briefly. To another writer it was Dec. 25, 1912, in Bond, Mississippi. This is Christmas Day, and Bond is where his wife, Patricia, was born. And to the third sportswriter Diz related it was Feb. 22, 1913, in Lucas, Arkansas. The last town was correct, but it's no more than one should expect when you admit to being born on Washington's birthday. It was another indication of Dizzy Dean's ability to "lay it on with a trowel" that he continued to maintain the friendship of all three writers.

Dizzy Dean's father, Albert Monroe Dean, was a tie hacker for the railroad when he met Alma Nelson in the little town of Barber, Arkansas, just around the turn of the century. They were married, settled in that area, and she bore him four sons: Charles (who died a year and half later), Elmer, Jay, and Paul.

Ab Dean, who was born in Rolla, Missouri, was a rabid baseball fan and a good semi-pro ball player. Someone who met Dizzy's father for the first time described him "as lookin' like a man whose cotton crop had been destroyed by the boll weevil ... who had lived on

Dean family collection, courtesy of Gene Kirby

In this 1929 game-action shot, Jay Dean, who was about to earn his nickname "Dizzy," is seen doing what he did best during his Army days - play baseball.

armadillo meat … whose house and barn had been blown away by an Oklahoma twister … and then the Depression hit!" Ab Dean was big, raw-boned and muscular. He worked the land most of his life and brought up his sons to do the same.

Dizzy's mother, Alma, also worked in the fields alongside her husband and children. Before the three boys were old enough to work, they would be taken to the field and put on a quilt at the end of a cotton row while Mom and Dad picked the crop. Sitting there at the end of the row doing nothing must have made a lasting impression on young Jay. After they became old enough to work in the fields, Jay would pay his brothers a penny or two out of what he earned to work his row for him. He sat and waited for them at the other end of the row! Even at such an early age, Jay Dean was thinking about how to get out of work. Alma Dean passed away when Jay was seven years old, and he always said he could remember it as though it was yesterday. Elmer, Paul and Jay were out in the orchard picking some

"early apples." They came back to the house to give some to their mother, but Dad Dean told them she was sleeping. Then, sitting them down in front of him on the top step, he told the boys she had died and they wouldn't be seeing her again.

The day of the funeral a line of mules, hacks and carriages stretched out for almost half a mile on the way to the cemetery at Pine Log, Arkansas. The boys were driven there in a wagon pulled by two mules. Diz remembered his Uncle Rutherford taking them by the hand and leading them to the grave where she was buried. Their mother was good to them, and she worked hard all her life. It wasn't easy working the way she did and trying to raise a family, too. She kept the three boys neat and clean, though they each owned just one pair of pants and a shirt. They only wore shoes "when the frost hit the ground."

They got to church on Sundays, and sometimes they even stayed for the preaching. "We ate well, too," remembered Dizzy, "even though we didn't have everything we would have liked to have

The state of Arkansas, especially the farming community of Lucas, was proud to claim the Dean brothers as favorite sons. This snapshot, printed in 1968, is believed to have been shot by the author or perhaps Dizzy Dean's wife, Pat.

had. Nothin' fancy, mind ya, jest good ol' fashioned cookin' with plenty of fried chicken, taters, ham, biscuits, an' red-eye gravy. That's why when we used to go to those county fairs and picnics, we'd always head straight for the tables that had the chocolate cakes and fruit pies.

We'd fill up on 'em 'cause we never got those things at home."

It was many years later that I learned what killed his mom was, as he said, "The COMPIL-ATIONS (complications) that set in a couple of weeks after she gave birth to a stillborn baby."

Shortly after Alma Dean's death, the family moved to Chickalah Mountain where Ab Dean took over raising the boys. "Dad was strict but fair with us," Dizzy said. "When it came time to get up in the mornin' to do our chores, all he had to do was grunt and that meant, 'hit the floor.' If you didn't, you felt the bottoms of his size 12s in a hurry. He whipped us, too. And we never regretted it either. He also taught us never to be run over, either. If we came home from school (which didn't happen too often 'cause we didn't go to school that much), and cried about someone hittin' us, he'd get mad and tell us to go back and whip that boy good – the one who done it. And if we didn't do it, he'd whip us again when we came home."

Ab Dean called his boys Piddle,

Poodle and Paul. Dizzy was Piddle because he was always piddling around – always getting into something. There was no telling what he'd do. Diz remembers going into a neighbor's watermelon patch with a couple of other kids and stealing some melons. When he got back home, Ab Dean had heard all about it. Well, besides getting a good whipping, his dad made Piddle sit down and start eating the melons until he got sick of the sight of them. Dizzy swore up and down that he'd never eat another piece of watermelon for the rest of his life.

Why the names Jay and Hanna? Jay was for a prominent member of an American family of financiers associated

Baseball popularity, unlike the economy, was booming in 1929. Fans gather at Fort Sam Houston in San Antonio, Texas to watch local teams compete for pride and cold beer.

with railroads – Jay Gould. The middle name of Hanna was for Marcus Alonzo Hanna, an American politician and well-to-do businessman from Ohio. Hanna helped make William McKinley president in 1896.

"Podnah," Dizzy would say, "I done everything I could to live up to the names and REPA-TATIONS (reputations) of them two gentlemen."

DEAN VS. U.S. ARMY (NO CONTEST!)

We reproach people for
Talking about themselves.
But, it is the subject they trust best.
Anatole France (1844-1924)

The story of Jay Hanna Dean's hitch in the peacetime U.S. Army back in the 1920s had to be the pilot for every movie or television show ever produced about a bungling, clumsy, maladjusted, unadapted, goofed-up, green-as-a-gourd soldier.

The TV antics of Sergeant Bilko and Gomer Pyle or the movie escapades of Laurel and Hardy and Abbott and Costello pale in comparison to the blue funk Jay Dean put the military into during his two-and-a-half years of service.

Jay Dean was recruited into the Army at Spaulding, Oklahoma, where his dad and two brothers, Elmer and Paul, were sharecropping on the Galimore Farm. Herman Parham, their stepbrother, was stationed at the Army Recruiting Office in Houston, Texas. While on furlough visiting the Deans, Herman talked Jay into enlisting.

There was, however, one slight problem. Jay was only 16 years old at the time. But that little problem was taken care of if his dad would give his consent. Just sign an affidavit saying that Jay was 18, and the problem was solved. The Army recruiter being kinfolk didn't hurt much either.

A check of Army records reveals that Jay Dean was permitted to enlist with the consent of his father, A.M. Dean. A notary in Hughes County, Oklahoma, declared that Jay was born in Holdenville, Oklahoma, that he stood 6-1 and weighed but 145 pounds. Jay Hanna Dean was now in the Army.

With only the clothes on his back and $16 in his pocket – his pay for picking cotton that fall – Jay Dean was driven to Houston. Passing his physical, he was assigned to the 3rd Wagon Company at Ft. Sam Houston in San Antonio, Texas.

The reason he wanted to join the Army?

"Now, there's nothing wrong with pickin' cotton," Dizzy would say later, " 'cause lots of people done it. But when I was a kid in Arkansas, I'd see them people drivin' them big cars, and they didn't have no more schoolin' than I did. I wondered how in the world if they could do it, why couldn't I do it, too?"

Dean had ambition, which is one reason he went into the Army. Jay also knew they played a lot of baseball in the Army, and that's what he really wanted to do. He figured if somebody saw him pitch, he might just get a chance to try out with the pros.

Jay Dean's first year and a half in the Army was uneventful as far as he was concerned. Transferred to Battery A of the 12th Field Artillery, Jay played some ball but only in pickup games. His unit did not field a team. Dean did, however, manage to pitch for a couple of semi-pro teams in the area. His pay? Anywhere from $1.50 to a couple of bottles of red soda pop each game. On this basis, Jay was already getting some recognition as a pretty good pitcher.

As a soldier, though, word was getting around that Jay Dean didn't take too kindly to any type of Army discipline. And he was the first to admit it. "Podnah," he said many times, "I was cut out to be a soldier, but I was sewed up wrong! I'd only signed up, so's I could play baseball. That's all I ever wanted to do. The Army didn't always see it that way. I wasn't a fella who wuz mean or hurt anybody. I was jest MIS-CHEEVUS (mischevious)."

"I didn't care whether I come out in the mornin' and stand revulla (reveille) with my leggin's wrapped up or not," he continued. "I'd sleep late and get up about five or 10 minutes after the bugle blowed. Then I'd jump up, put on my leggin's, not even wrappin' 'em up and run out draggin' 'em behind me. The officer would come by, take one look at me, and, sure enough, he'd write me up.

And back I would go on to KP (kitchen police) or stable police."

That's where Jay Dean spent most of his time while he was in the Army. "But there was no harm in that," he said. "Somebody had to wash them dishes and clean up them horses. That was my job. Every mornin' all the soldiers would go up to the bulletin board to see who was on KP or the stable police. Sure enough, there was my name at the top of the list. I jest couldn't obey them Army orders or any kind of orders. I been that way all my life."

Dean's chores in the stables consisted of cleaning up the stalls and taking care of the ponies after the officers had finished playing polo. He was on duty one day when an order came in that one of the officers needed some fertilizer for his garden. It was to be sent over right away; time passed and the order still hadn't been filled. The officer went down to the stables to see about it. Spotting Pvt. Dean, the officer asked about the order and wanted to know why it hadn't been delivered. Checking the list very

carefully, Dean said to the officer, "Sir, you got nothing to worry about. Your name is right here. You're next on my s--- list!" Dean's ears blistered for a week!

In January, 1928, Jay Dean was transferred to Battery C of the 12th Field Artillery. It was a horse-drawn outfit headed by 1st Sgt. James K. "Jimmy" Brought, who was also the manager of the Army post baseball team. The tough, little sergeant has a special niche reserved for himself in any book, story or article ever written about Jay Janna Dean. It was Jimmy Brought who gave Dean the nickname Dizzy. The name now has a certain degree of affection to it when spoken by friends and fans. But when Sgt. Brought used the word Dizzy for the first time to the young buck private, it was anything but that.

One day, beside himself with rage at the complete lack of respect for Army discipline shown by Dean in his various jobs on the post, the sergeant yelled, "Private Dean, you're as dizzy as you look!" And Brought repeated it several times. In the peacetime Army soldiers trained without live ammunition. On more than one occasion, Sgt. Brought could be heard shouting at Dean, "You dizzy S.O.B.! If this .45 pistol of mine was loaded with live ammo, I'd shoot you in the ass 45 times even if you are the best damn pitcher on the team!"

No shots were ever fired, but the nickname stuck.

Dizzy always claimed that he never made more than private while in the Army. The records, however, show that he did get promoted to private first class … but only for 12 days. Then he was busted back to private. The reason? His outfit, the 12th Field Artillery, hauled the big French .75 millimeter guns. These .75s were pulled by three teams of horses, two to a team, with a soldier riding one of the horses. There was a lead team, a swing team and a wheel team. Dean's job was to handle the wheel team, and his two horses were named Bobby and Goofy.

Dean family collection, courtesy of Gene Kirby

Jay Dean was not much of a soldier, but his pitching skills were in high demand. Here, the guy his Army sergeant called "Dizzy" (top row, second from right), is playing with a team from New Braunfels, which led to a pro tryout and a contract with the St. Louis Cardinals.

On maneuvers one hot afternoon, the order was given to get rolling. Out of the shed came the lead team and the swing team right in line followed by the wheel team. Suddenly, the wheel team of Dizzy, Bobby and Goofy on a command from Dizzy cut too sharply and crashed into the main support pole. Down came the shed, and it landed on the equipment, horses and men, putting a stop to the maneuvers, temporarily … and busting Dean back to private … PERMANENTLY!

Later that day, Sgt. Brought, when discussing the matter of Pvt. Dean with his commanding officer, said, "Sir, Dean is really a good boy. He'll do anything in the world you ask him to do. The only bad thing about it is that you have to tell him so damn many times!"

Whatever shortcomings Dean may have had as a representative soldier in Uncle Sam's Army, he more than made up for it on the baseball diamond. He loved to play ball, and he could throw hard! Sgt. Brought once said, "Dizzy was a natural. He absorbed baseball quickly. He gave the fans a real show with that exaggerated windmill windup, and he packed the stands every time he pitched."

In March 1929 while on maneuvers at Camp Stanley, Texas, Dean walked up to Sgt. Brought and asked to see the commanding officer. "What the hell for?" asked the sergeant. "Sir," Dizzy told him, "I want to make a purchase." In those days, even though you had enlisted for three years in the peacetime Army, you could buy your way out for $100. This was what was meant by a purchase.

Sgt. Brought just laughed. "Where in the hell are you going to get the money to buy your way out?" he said. "You haven't got 10 cents, let alone $100." Dean retorted, "Yes, I have!" Dizzy proceeded to show Brought five $20 bills that he said had been given to him by his father. At the time, Ab Dean was living near the Army base on Rattlesnake Hill in San Antonio with Dizzy's brother Paul.

Where did Diz actually get the money? His dad said he paid it. Brother Paul said he paid it. The San Antonio Public Service Company also said it provided the bucks. A semi-pro team for which Dizzy often pitched said it put up the money. Take your pick. Dizzy Dean had a different story every time the subject came up in a conversation.

There was a problem, however, before Dean could get out of the Army. The sergeant in charge told Dizzy that before he could issue discharge papers, Dean would have to turn in all clothing and equipment issued by the government since he had joined.

Diz had no idea what he had been issued. He knew he didn't have a mess kit because, as he said, "I never ate out of them any way. I jes' used 'em for when they inspected us." But Dean found a way out of the jam. He asked the sergeant for a list of things he had been issued, and left the office.

Going back to the barracks, Dean quickly went down the rows of bunks and grabbed shirts, a pair of shoes, mess kit, hat, pants, leggings, and anything else on the list that belonged to the other soldiers. Stuffing it all into a duffel bag, he returned to the office and dumped it all on the sergeant's desk. "Here ya are, sir," he said. "Everything you wanted is right here. Now give me my purchase."

"In 1934 when I won those 30 games for the Cardinals and two more in the World Series, " Dizzy said later. "In other words, when I got to be a suss-sess (success), the U.S. Army came out with them big recruiting posters … you know the ones where they show Uncle Sam pointing' at ya. Well, they had my picture on them posters! Can ya believe it? And they said, 'Join the Army! The U.S. Army trained him! It can do the same for you!' Now ain't that a laugh!"

Two years later, Dizzy Dean went back to San Antonio to attend a reunion of his 12th Field Artillery buddies. All the boys began talking about Dean's escapades that they said made Ol' Diz a military legend.

These remarks got a quick response from Sgt. Brought, who jumped up and shouted, "Legend my ass! That damn Dean was a menace!"

FIRST PRO CONTRACT
★

Dizzy Dean's youth became so shrouded in myth and baseball legend, even the date he inked his first pro contract remains a bit fuzzy. We just know that Dizzy signed in 1930. Maybe.

Dean family collection, courtesy of Gene Kirby

The Texas League

of

Professional Baseball Clubs

has awarded to

Jerome Herman Dean

Pitcher of the Houston Baseball Club

recognition as the most valuable all-round player in the service of any one club during the season of

1931

Once Dizzy Dean signed with St. Louis, he pitched his way through the Cardinals farm system, in short order. In his second season as a pro, Dizzy, then with the Houston Buffs, was named MVP of the storied Texas League. By then, Dizzy had managed to purposely confuse people into using his "other" name.

The influential and historically accurate Baseball Reference website (baseballreference.com) only lists 1930, with no firm date attached. Even this leading authority on the national past-time attaches a side note, asserting that the actual date may be in question.

Many baseball historians were swayed, however, when the group Robert Edward Auctions produced what is believed to be an authenticated, four-page contract between the Houston Buffs (a St. Louis Cardinals Class AA franchise) and Dizzy on Aug. 2, 1930. The document, labeled "Professional Base Ball Player's Uniform Contract," sold at auction in 2011 for $2,644. Note the two-word legal usage of "Base Ball" (two words) – used on such contracts dating back to the horse-and-buggy days of the 1890s. Other historians say Dean actually signed a contract with Houston earlier that summer of 1930, on an unknown date, before he was optioned down to Class C St. Joseph of the Western League.

In any case, the "original" Houston document was a four-page folded contract between Dizzy and the Houston Baseball Association, containing black fountain pen signatures of both J. H. Dean and Fred N. Ankenman (president of the Buffaloes from 1925-43). For ballplayers of the day, the game was hardly a get-rich-quick proposition.

Dizzy's one-year agreement with the minor league Buffs paid him $350 per month. Riches, along with national fame, would have to wait. – *Bo Carter*

NOT LONG FOR THE MINORS

★

Dizzy Dean's minor league career was the envy of many at the time (1930 and '31) and would be almost unbelievable in these modern days of pitch counts and clubs developing their prized prospects slowly and with great care. While Dizzy plowed through his apprenticeship in the Cardinals chain in short order, today a young pitcher – even one with Major League talent – could expect to ride plenty of buses and eat lots of box lunches as he progressed through 3-4 classifications and rookie leagues. Not Dizzy.

Dizzy's mighty right arm was no stranger to workload when the former farm boy reported to St. Joseph, Missouri, some 45 miles from Kansas City in the pitching-heavy Western League. After signing with the Houston Buffaloes, Dizzy worked just over a month toward the Labor Day regular-season finale, posting an 8-2 record with a 2.86 earned run average. It was a busy month, starting nine games, and appearing in five others out of the bullpen. After his minor league duty was finished in Houston, there was no rest in sight.

On Sept. 28, 1930, after a one-game call-up to the Cardinals, Dizzy made his Major League debut with a sterling, three-hit, 3-1 victory over Pittsburgh. The kid from the cotton fields showed he was just about ready for the big stage.

While writers and teammates raved

about his potential, Cardinals general manager Branch Rickey and field manager Gabby Street were not enamored with Dizzy's brash behavior, then-unheard of for a rookie. As the big club headed north out of spring training just prior to the 1931 campaign, Cardinals execs gave the swaggering right-hander a quick train ticket back to Houston. Dean did anything but sulk and pout.

Dizzy responded with workhorse effort, leading the Buffs to a Texas League title. That season's slash: 26-10 record, 304 innings pitched, 41 total appearances, 32 starting assignments, and led the Buffs to a Texas League title. He clinched the League crown by pitching and winning both ends of a doubleheader.

As was becoming his custom, Dizzy made a name for himself off the diamond, too.

In keeping with his antics with St. Joseph the year before, Dizzy left field manager Joe Schultz and team president Fred Ankenman of Houston with a trail of clothing store and sporting goods bills,

plus restaurant tabs, far beyond his monthly base salary of $350.

While gouging management off the field, Dizzy more than pulled his weight on the mound. His two-year minor league record of 51-20 covered 606 innings, in 87 total games, including 64 starts. His whopping 606 innings pitched would not be duplicated by a Cardinal farmhand for the next 84 seasons. – *Bo Carter*

Dizzy Dean was still a teenager when this 1929 photo was taken of him in a uniform issued by City Public Service, the major utility firm in San Antonio, Texas. Research indicates the photo was shot downtown, not far from the Alamo, behind where the now-defunct San Antonio Light was once published.

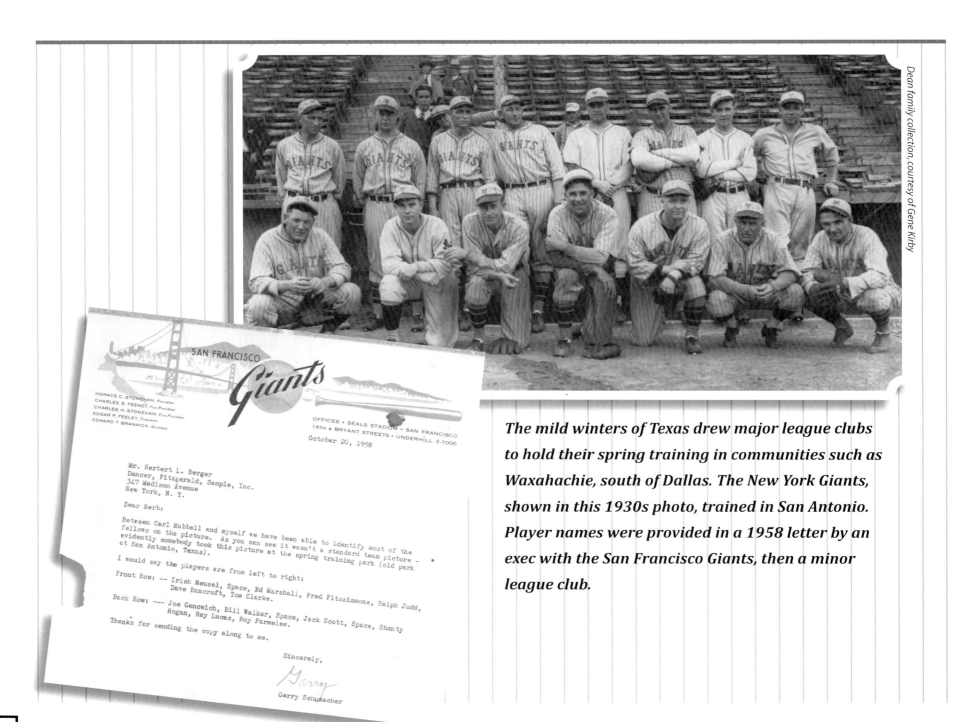

SAN FRANCISCO

Giants

HORACE C. STONEHAM, *President*
CHARLES S. FEENEY, *Vice President*
CHARLES H. STONEHAM, *Vice President*
EDGAR P. FEELEY, *Treasurer*
EDWARD T. BRANNICK, *Secretary*

OFFICES • SEALS STADIUM • SAN FRANCISCO
16TH & BRYANT STREETS • UNDERHILL 3-7000

October 20, 1958

Mr. Herbert L. Berger
Dancer, Fitzgerald, Sample, Inc.
347 Madison Avenue
New York, N. Y.

Dear Herb:

Between Carl Hubbell and myself we have been able to identify most of the
fellows on the picture. As you can see it wasn't a standard team picture --
evidently somebody took this picture at the spring training park (old park
at San Antonio, Texas).

I would say the players are from left to right:

Front Row: -- Irish Meusel, Space, Ed Marshall, Fred Fitzsimmons, Ralph Judd,
Dave Bancroft, Tom Clarke.

Back Row: --- Joe Genowich, Bill Walker, Space, Jack Scott, Space, Shanty
Hogan, Ray Lucas, Roy Parmelee.

Thanks for sending the copy along to me.

Sincerely,

Garry

Garry Schumacher

The mild winters of Texas drew major league clubs to hold their spring training in communities such as Waxahachie, south of Dallas. The New York Giants, shown in this 1930s photo, trained in San Antonio. Player names were provided in a 1958 letter by an exec with the San Francisco Giants, then a minor league club.

Dean family collection, courtesy of Gene Kirby

Decades after a brief brush with formal education, Dizzy Dean returned to Lucas, Arkansas, where he found his third-grade teacher, Ralph Dennis. This photo is believed to have been shot, perhaps by Dizzy's wife, Pat, in the late 1960s. By then, Dizzy was a national TV personality.

Dean family collection, courtesy of Gene Kirby

As early as 1930, when Dizzy Dean hunted geese with friend Oliver French near Charleston, Missouri, the pitcher loved his hunting and fishing.

The legend varies with the telling, but research shows that Jay Dean got his nickname from U.S. Army Sgt. Jimmy Brought (above right). Though Dizzy was a mediocre soldier at best, he returned to Fort Sam Houston in 1936, having emerged as a national celebrity and the dominant right-hander of his era.

Part III

Playing Days

DIZZY — PLAYING AS FEW EVER HAVE

It doesn't take a backhoe, or even a garden spade, to dig through Dizzy Dean's earliest baseball lore. Stories – some of them true, some pure fabrication – are everywhere, even decades after the fact. But by all reliable accounts, Dizzy buzzed through his formative years like a big league heater right under the batter's chin.

Once he joined the U.S. Army, Dean got three squares a day, all right, but his "service" is most remembered for slipping

Blessed with a rangy, athletic frame and a strong arm, Dizzy Dean put those tools to work with an iron will to win. This 1933 sequence from Sportsman's Park in St. Louis shows a free-wheeling delivery - but the taped thumb would not be allowed today.

off base on weekends. Dizzy pitched for or against San Antonio-area semi-pro town teams in New Braunfels, Comfort, Medina, Fredericksburg, Kerrville and Boerne. Good as he was on the mound, Pvt. Jay Dean RA 6 233 400 just might be the worst soldier in Fort Sam Houston history.

"He loved to play (baseball)," Sgt. James K. Brought once said of his famous, slipshod private. "That's all he lived for. He never got enough."

Word of the long-limbed right-hander with a laser beam fastball got around, leading to a telegram from Mickey Cochrane inviting him to try out with the Tigers, and another from Rogers Hornsby with the old St. Louis Browns. Dizzy was prime to ditch his fatigues, so he used $140 he won shooting craps (some say) to buy his way out of the Army. Buyouts were not uncommon in those days, but Dizzy's fastball was anything but ordinary. Scout Don Curtis signed Dizzy to a Cardinals contract, assigning him to the club's Texas League farm team in Houston. Salary: $300. No signing bonus.

The date was March 1930. Mark it well. Baseball history was about to change.

Dizzy would bounce back and forth from Houston to the big club in St. Louis, rollicking along, entertaining the press, making friends and foes along the way. Then, the pace begins to quicken.

In short order, Dizzy marries Patricia Nash (1931) and gets called up to the Cardinals to stay (1932). By 1934, Pat establishes herself as the Alpha female, Dizzy's keeper and a lingering hangnail for team management. Meanwhile, the former sharecropper emerges as the dominant right-hander in the game, posting a 30-7 record and winning two World Series games against Detroit. Hitters dig in on Dizzy, only at their own peril.

Judging from his arm angle in period photos, Dizzy's famous fastball – "my fogger," he called it – must have been a bat-buster, sinking like a brick and boring in on the thumbs of right-handers. When Diz thought a message needed to be delivered, he notoriously would elevate a purpose pitch, sending the would-be hitter sprawling in the dust. This was before batting helmets, remember.

Ruling over his domain, Dizzy Dean was a land shark, not a real estate shyster, but a top-tier baseball predator with a toothy fastball and yappy jaws. His unapologetic approach led to contract disputes, benches-emptying brawls, and even clubhouse feuds with teammates after he bad-mouthed them in the press. His frequent threats to jump the team sold newspapers, but also stirred the cauldron of team chemistry. By all accounts, Dizzy kept his own counsel (except with Pat), and alternately could be a colossal jackass, or the toast of baseball, sometimes both on the same day.

Celebratory champagne turns to vinegar, however, when a line drive breaks his toe and ultimately alters Dizzy's free-wheeling delivery. The injury and overwork – he pitched in relief between starts – combine to douse the flame from his feared heater. No longer the mound master, Dizzy retires to a radio-TV broadcast career that makes him wealthy, boosts his considerable ego and adds to his bigger-than-life reputation.

In 1947, bragging that he could still get big league hitters out, Dizzy forsakes the press box one last time. Pitching around a flabby belly, sure enough, he tosses four scoreless innings. At age 37, Dizzy at long last leaves the diamond to younger men. But even then, "ol' Diz," as he calls himself, is not finished.

For more than a quarter century to come, Dizzy Dean's influence on the game, his TV work with Falstaff and Gene Kirby, along with his thumbprint on American culture, would grow ever bigger and taller, far, far beyond the chalk lines. – *Mark S. McDonald*

DIZZY TIES THE KNOT – THAT NEVER COMES UNDONE

It sits in a prominent corner of Finger Furniture on what is now Gulf Freeway near downtown Houston, Texas. Graybeards with a memory might say it's where long-gone Buff Stadium was home for the old Houston Buffaloes (1928-1961), before Major League Baseball expanded in 1961 to include the Houston Colt .45s.

Contrary to legend, Buff Stadium was *not* also the site of the 1931 wedding of Dizzy Dean and local sales clerk Patricia Nash. Repeat, not.

The Dean couple was said to have said their vows at home plate, amidst crossed bats of Buff teammates. Makes a good story, but it never happened that way, says long-time Dizzy Dean sidekick and partner in fun, Gene Kirby.

"Pat Dean would not have stood for a wedding at home plate at a minor league stadium," Kirby always said. "She wanted a church wedding with all the trimmings."

Dean family collection, courtesy of Gene Kirby

Once Dizzy Dean married the former Patricia Nash, she quickly asserted herself in handling the couple's finances. Her role - to the disdain of Dizzy's baseball employers - extended to contract negotiations.

The June 15, 1931, ceremony at Pat's home church – First Christian – was a traditional double ring ceremony at the second home of the congregation on Main and Bell Streets just west of downtown Houston.

Truth took a further beating when at least three accounts – including the critically panned movie "Pride of St. Louis" – portrayed the Buffs' public relations director (another name, which has vanished) as orchestrating a home-plate ceremony. It, too, never occurred.

Such a blatant publicity stunt would have strained credulity but for Dean's instant and immense popularity. In just two seasons, however, the young right-hander was so good and so freshly outspoken, he was a boon to the St. Louis farm club and all its Texas League rivals. Wherever Dizzy pitched, he boosted sales and made new baseball fans, even as the tight-money Great Depression closed its grip on America's windpipe.

Today, printed proceedings and guest list from the Dean wedding service eluded research. And time eventually caught up with First Christian Church.

The Church in 2004 was rebuilt at 1601 Sunset Lane, just off Main, a half-mile from the Bayou City's Rice University campus. In a leafy neighborhood shaded by live oaks dating back to Texas' days as an independent republic, First Christian is a grand and peaceful structure, a place with a past. – *Bo Carter*

Both on the diamond and off, Paul Dean (left) could always count on the rapid support of his older brother, Dizzy.

HE'P IN THE OUTFIELD

"**A** lot of fans always asked me if I ever called in the outfield and then struck out the side with those players standing around the infield," Dizzy said. "Well, there's no way that ever happened. Why, I needed all the he'p I could get when I wuz pitchin'. Besides, you can't do things like that in PERFESSIONAL (professional) ball. That would be makin' a FAR-SICAL (farce) outta the game!

"What I did do one time in Houston in 1931 in the Texas League was walk three batters IN TEN-SI-CAL (intentional) like, ya know, on purpose," he added, "to load the bases so I could pitch to the Dallas catcher, Al Todd.

"Now Todd and me had been in a fight a month before," Dean noted. "I'd knocked him down, and when he got up he yelled something to me, so I knocked him down again! Well, he dropped the bat and started walkin' to the mound. I figured he wuz gonna talk it over with me first. Before I knowed it, he hit me right on the jaw and down I went. I got up, and he whacked me again, and down I went again. That really started a ruckus. To tell the truth, I wasn't much of a fighter.

"A couple of years later my brother, Paul, was also pitching for the Cardinals," he continued. "Todd was now catching for the Phillies. Now Paul knew all about what happened between me and Todd in the Texas League. But he wuzn't like Ol' Diz. Paul was as 'rough as a cob' and twice as mean."

One of Dizzy Dean's favorite Cardinals teammates was infielder Pepper Martin. In 1933, long before weight training or muscle-building steroids, the rough-and-ready Martin shows off his physique during spring training in Bradenton, Florida.

"Well, Todd came up to bat," Dizzy said, "and on the first pitch Paul turned him upside down with a fastball under the whiskers. I mean he 'undressed' him. He hit the dirt, got up, yelled something out to Paul, and started walking toward the mound. Paul took off his glove, walked toward the plate, and yelled, 'Keep walkin', Al! This ain't Ol' Diz y'alls (bleeping) around with!' Todd turned around and went back to the plate. That was the last of it. They didn't mess around too much with Paul."

PEPPER MARTIN

One winter, Dizzy and teammate Pepper Martin, known as the "Wild Hoss of the Osage," were invited guests at the annual prison rodeo held in the state penitentiary in Huntsville, Texas. Of the many events in this unique competition between inmates, the calf-roping contest most intrigued the visiting ballplayers.

Cowboys would ride out after a calf, lasso it, get off the horse, wrestle the calf to the ground, and tie up its hind legs. The time it took would then be announced to the crowd. Before anyone knew it, Ol' Diz in street clothes had talked his way into participating in the event.

Mounting a borrowed horse, Dizzy came thundering out of the gate and took off in hot pursuit of the calf. He tried to lasso the calf three times, and three times he missed. The crowd was roaring at the spectacle.

Finally, Diz roped the calf, got off the horse, wrestled the calf to the ground, and tied it up. The crowd went wild, giving the pitcher a standing ovation!

"Ladies and gentlemen," the announcement came over the loudspeakers, "that was the great Dizzy Dean. The time for Mr. Dean ... (pause) he had a helluva time!"

DIZZY AND FRISCH: PART ONE

Dizzy and Hall of Fame player and Cardinals' manager Frankie Frisch had their share of differences of opinion, to say the least.

"Frankie Frisch came out to the mound one time when he thought I was in some kind of trouble," Ol' Diz said, "which I wuzn't.

"He started sweet talkin' to me. 'Now, Jerome, he would say, be careful with this guy. Pitch him low and away. No curves, just fastballs ... Don't give him anything too good to hit ... but don't walk him!'"

This encouragement generally met with a chilly reception. Dean always had the same reply:

"I hear what y'alls sayin', Frank, but why don't I jest strike his ass out!" And the determined right-hander would do just that, on three pitches!

Dizzy Dean and his driven manager, Frankie Frisch, had a storied and sometimes stormy working relationship.

CONTRACT DISPUTES

Contract negotiations between the Deans and the advertising agency and the brewery, Falstaff, were always long, drawn-out battles. Usually they went public, creating major headlines in the daily papers. These "negotiations," if you could call them that, were made even more acrimonious because of Dizzy's determination to agitate the living hell out of everyone involved.

One year, holding out for $100,000 a year and a long-term contract, Dean threatened to quit the baseball broadcasts and the brewery if he didn't get what he wanted. Broadcast contracts always were haggled out with the advertising agency, which then got Falstaff's approval. Agency people were tougher to deal with – which made Ol' Diz much more obstinate.

These talks had been going on for a long time. They not only involved more money but also deferred payments, personal appearances, vacation time during the baseball season, and Patricia Dean's travel

Dizzy Dean's behavior and contract squabbles sometimes wound up at baseball's highest levels. In this 1930s meeting, Cardinals manager Frank Frisch (left) sits with a disgruntled Dizzy, Major League Baseball Commissioner Judge Kennesaw Mountain Landis and Jim Breadon.

expenses. Unusual for the day, she went along with Dizzy on almost every trip.

Finally, Dizzy had enough of all this bickering and made a suggestion. "I'll work for one year for just $100,000," he stated, "but I want all my money in cash and in one lump sum!"

At this point, Patricia came into the conversation. "Why, Jay, that's crazy!" she shouted. "In that case you'll have to give most of the money to the government! Why not spread the payments out?"

"I don't care," Diz countered. "Tell you what I'm gonna do. I'll take the 100,000 bucks, go back home to our ranch in Texas, buy $100,000 worth of cow manure, and spread it all over our 140 acres.

"Then I'm gonna call the Internal Revenue Service in Washington and tell 'em to go ahead and take whatever I owe 'em right out of it!"

Needless to say, Mrs. Dean was unmoved. As was so often the case, she eventually won out and the Dean couple opted for the more traditional way of getting paid.

REVERSING CHARGES

Talking to a reporter in Florida one day, Dean excused himself, saying he needed to make a phone call. He was gone for quite a while and finally came back grinning.

Dizzy Dean enjoys a light moment with Cardinals General Manager Branch Rickey and team manager Frankie Frisch. Dizzy loved to aggravate club administration.

"Well," he said, "I just called Mr. Breadon (the Cardinals owner) in St. Louis and told him I changed my mind and that I wasn't gonna sign my contract for $20,000.

"We had a big argument, yelled back and forth for about 20 minutes, and he threatened to have me thowed out of baseball! He was really hot. Then I told him that I had done signed my contract and sent it back to him in the mail."

"Diz," the reporter asked, "why in hell would you want to do that?"

Ol' Diz just laughed. "Podnah," he replied, "I was just agitatin' him. I even had the (long-distance phone) charges reversed, and it cost him $23!"

Dean family collection, courtesy of Gene Kirby

A LITTLE CHIN MUSIC

★

"They're not hitters 'til they get a hit offen ya!" Dizzy Dean often said. "And there's no harm in playin' a little 'chin music' with 'em."

Facing a batter who had not gotten a hit off him in two years, Ol' Diz fired his fastball, and the batter swung and fouled off the pitch. His next pitch almost "de-horned" the hitter. The batsman's cap went one way, the bat went up in the air,

Though he denied it, Dizzy Dean - like many pitchers of the era - was not above throwing dangerously close to a hitter, just to push him off the plate.

and the batter went down on his back.

"His toes wuz pointed up towards the sky!" Dean always liked to say. Of course, when questioned by an umpire or league officials, Dizzy always denied *ever* throwing at a batter.

Getting back to his feet and visibly shaken, the batter yelled at Dizzy. "What the hell are you throwing me, you big SOB," he shouted. "I ain't had a hit off of you in two years."

"I know it, Podnah," Ol' Diz hollered back, "but you just swung real hard and fouled off that pitch ... and it looked like you might be gettin' to me!"

DIGGING IN ON DIZZY

When it came to throwing at hitters, which Dizzy Dean denied ever doing, the right-hander had his own code of conduct.

"One thing that always upset me was when those doggone hitters would start diggin' in at home plate," the old pitcher would say. "That's because they wanted to get a good 'toe-holt' to hit the ball. Ya see, I always pitched fast. I didn't mess around and shake my catcher off two or three times."

On the mound, Dizzy could be strictly business.

"I didn't step off the rubber, then step on it a couple of times before firing away. I was ready to thow the minute I got the ball back from my catcher.

"Then the umpire would call time to give the batter more chance to keep diggin'. That *really* got me mad."

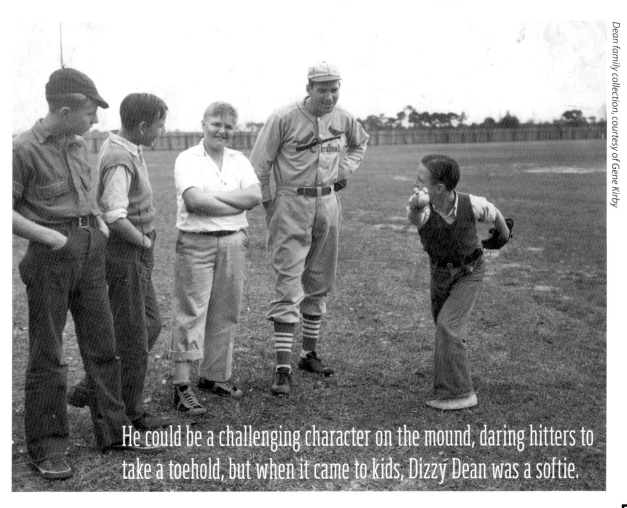

He could be a challenging character on the mound, daring hitters to take a toehold, but when it came to kids, Dizzy Dean was a softie.

Soon enough, the hitter is comfortable in the batter's box and the umpire points to Dizzy.

"Okay," the ump says, "now pitch!"

Dizzy would be something less than pleased.

"That's when I would call time and walk to home plate and say to the hitter: 'Okay, Podnah, y'all finished diggin'? If not, keep on diggin' and dig yourself a deep hole 'cause with my next pitch I'm gonna bury your ass right in that hole!'"

Note: today they call that "trash talking!"

NOT ON THE HIT LIST

T hough he always denied it to umpires, Dizzy had no qualms about throwing at batters. But the big pitcher did have some friends in the game, ballplayers he never knocked down. Among them were Burgess Whitehead of the Cardinals and Billy Herman of the

Cubs – both former teammates.

After being traded to the New York Giants, Whitehead came up to bat against Ol' Diz in a game at the Polo Grounds. On the first pitch Burgess lined a ball right back to the mound and hit Dean, as Dizzy recalled it during a broadcast, "right in the lowest part of my back!"

Selective with his high, hard ones at a batter's head, Dizzy Dean made lasting friendships with 1933 Cardinals teammates Jim Bottomly, Bill Hallahan and (right) Jimmy Wilson. The famed Gashouse Gang was taking shape.

Whitehead shocked everybody in the park by running right out to the mound to see if Dizzy had been hurt! He never ran to first base and, of course, was called out for running out of the baseline.

CLOSE CALL FOR HERMAN

★

One afternoon St. Louis was playing the Chicago Cubs. Cards Manager Frankie Frisch came over to Dizzy Dean before the game, in which he was the starting pitcher.

"Jerome," Frisch said, using a name Dizzy had adopted long after birth, "you've got to knock Billy Herman on his ass. He's been beating our brains out."

Herman was the Cubs' second baseman and a very good hitter. Ol' Diz didn't want to do it because of his friendship with Herman, and he told Frisch he wouldn't do it. But Frisch insisted.

So Dizzy got in touch with Billy before the game and told him what he had to do. Dean didn't want to knock him down or hit Herman with a pitch, but the manager told him to do it.

"Awww, Diz," Billy told his friendly rival, "you're not going to do it, are you?"

"Billy, I'm sorry, but I gotta!"

Herman, batting second in the Cubs lineup, came up in the first inning. Dean threw four fastballs, high and inside right, at Herman's head. Billy hit the dirt four times and then walked to first base. As Herman stood on first base, he looked over at Dizzy and started laughing. Dean didn't like that.

Dizzy toed the rubber and went into his stretch, checking Herman at first base. Then he wheeled around and fired the ball to first, zapping Herman, who had taken a couple of steps off the bag, right in the ribs. Direct hit.

"I done told ya I wuz gonna hit ya, Billy," Ol' Diz shouted, as the base-runner writhed in pain, "and I don't 'PRECIATE (appreciate) you laughin' at me!"

Courtesy of the National Baseball Hall of Fame, Cooperstown, New York

Dizzy Dean in his prime could be a clever pitcher. But in the 1934 World Series, Detroit left-hander Schoolboy Rowe was his near equal.

Lefty Grove was a veteran "wrong-hander" when he met the Cardinals' up-and-coming Dizzy Dean during Florida spring training in 1933. Grove would go on to win 300 games in 17 Hall of Fame seasons with Philadelphia and, later, Boston.

DEAN AND AL SPOHRER

★

One of Dizzy Dean's friends in baseball was Al Spohrer, a big burly catcher with the Boston Braves. On a trip to Braves Field late in the 1932 season, Dizzy found out that Judge Emil Fuchs, the Braves owner, had promised Spohrer a $250 bonus if he hit .275 for the season. Dizzy was not always charitable even to teammates, much less opponents, but on this occasion he looked up Spohrer before the game he was going to pitch.

"Podnah," Ol' Diz related, "I ain't gonna thow you nuthin' but fastballs right down the middle of the plate. Now get yoursef a couple of base hits, and that'll hep you get that bonus. Besides, both of our clubs is out of the pennant race."

Well, the first three times at bat Spohrer grounded out to the second baseman, flied out to the centerfielder and fouled out to the third baseman. Dizzy was now very upset as Spohrer came up to hit for the fourth and what could have been his last at-bat in the game.

Dizzy threw his first pitch, and Spohrer fouled it off behind the plate. It was a high foul, and both the umpire and Cardinals catcher went back to the screen to make sure the ball didn't hit the screen. That gave Dizzy time to run in toward home plate. "Podnah, **bunt** the damn ball," he told Spohrer, "and I'll fall down trying to field it, and you'll get yourself that base hit!"

When play was resumed, Dizzy fired another fastball right over the plate. The Braves catcher bunted the ball perfectly down the third baseline. Ol' Diz came off the mound, reached for the ball, missed it cleanly, and fell down. Dean was smart enough to know that if he touched the ball, the official scorer would rule it an error, not a hit for Spohrer.

Now on his knees, Dizzy reached for the ball again, picked it up, wheeled and fired it to first base. The moment Dean let the ball go, a big roar went up from the crowd! Spohrer had fallen down on his way to first base, and the ball beat him to the bag!

"Well, I tried my best, Podnah," Ol' Diz said later. "That's all a mule can do!"

DIZZY AND BILL KLEM

During one game Dizzy got into an argument with Hall of Fame umpire Bill Klem when he was called out on a close play at first base. They argued nose to nose for a couple of minutes when suddenly Dean fell flat on his back and lay there motionless as though he had just been shot.

The Cardinal players rushed out of their dugout and gathered around him. A call went out for a doctor in the ballpark. Everyone was deeply concerned that Dizzy was seriously hurt, or that he maybe had a heart attack.

Milling around the circles of players, Klem looked on for about 10 minutes, and then he had seen enough. He made his way through several players surrounding

Dean family collection, courtesy of Gene Kirby

By 1934, the St. Louis Cardinals Gas House Gang earned its nickname with a hell-bent approach that did not spare umpires. Left to right are Dizzy Dean, Leo Durocher, Ernie Orsatti, Bill DeLancey, Rip Collins, Joe Medwick, manager Frank Frisch, Jack Rothrock and Pepper Martin.

Ol' Diz, pushed them aside, looked down at the pitcher, playing possum.

"Dean," Klem bellowed, "dead or alive, you're out of the ballgame!"

ARGUING WITH UMPIRE GEORGE BARR

During one game Dizzy Dean got into a big argument with umpire George Barr. They yelled at each other for a few minutes, then Barr took off and walked down the right field line, followed by Dizzy, still jawing.

"George, talk to me," Dean said. "I'm askin' you a question about the play, and you ain't sayin' nuthin'!"

Barr stopped and turned around to face the pitcher.

"Dizzy, I *did* answer your question," Barr said. "Didn't you see me shake my head?"

Dean was quick with a reply.

"You did?" asked Ol' Diz. "Well, how come I didn't hear nuthin' rattle?"

Barr threw him out of the game on the spot!

GREAT DAY ON THE MOUND

One day I asked Dizzy Dean if he would tell me what was his best day out on the mound.

"Podnah," he answered, "I had a lot of great days. One of them was the day I struck out 17 Chicago Cubs. Now, that was no OR-NOR-EY (ordinary) game. That was in July 1933. It certainly didn't start out bein' a big day for me.

"Heck, "right in the very first innin' I give up a couple of hits, and we were losin' 1-0 before we even come to bat. Our manager, Frankie Frisch, hadn't been with us too long 'cause he had two guys warmin' up in the bullpen."

Frisch didn't know what his pitcher had in store.

"I coulda struck out more that day," Dizzy added, "but I didn't know nuthin' about no record. I was jest pitchin' away with Jimmie Wilson catchin' and he never said nuthin' about no record. Nobody else said a word about it either. I might even have broke the record for strikeouts in a row if somebody hadda told me what I was doin'.

In his Hall of Fame career, Dizzy Dean enjoyed many a grand day on the mound. This spring training day in the mid-1930s was just a tune-up. To his right are Leo Durocher, Don Gutteridge and catcher Spud Davis.

"Anyway, I strikes out the side in the fifth, eighth and ninth innings. Twelve of them hitters outta the 17 total I struck out went down swinging. I never done bothered pitchin' high or low when I was feelin' good. I jest fired my fastball in there right over the plate."

The ninth inning was especially memorable.

"I'll never forget that last innin'," Dean said. "Charley Grimm, the Cubs manager, sends up a pinch hitter. His name was Jim Mosolf. My catcher Jimmie Wilson meets this guy before he ever gets to the plate and tells me later what he said to Mosolf."

"Kid," Wilson said, "this is a helluva spot to put you in. I wouldn't be surprised if that 'dizzy guy' out there on the mound throws the first one right at your ear 'cause he doesn't like pinch hitters!"

Dizzy went on to say that Mosolf never took the bat off his shoulder.

"Wilson give me a sign," Ol' Diz said, "and then he'd straighten up and pound his fist into his glove right behind Mosolf's ear. The guy thought surer-'n-hell he was

gonna get one under his chin. I fired three pitches at him, Dean specials, right through there with the smoke curlin' off 'em, and he was gone."

Dean chuckled at the memory.

"That, Podnah, was jest one more of my greatest days!"

DEAN AND BOB FELLER

On July 6, 1936, Bob Feller pitched in an exhibition game against the St. Louis Cardinals at League Park in Cleveland. It was the first time Feller ever had hurled against a Major League team. Bob was only 17 years old, property of the Cleveland Indians, but he was pitching that day for the Cleveland Rosenblooms, a semi-pro club.

Before the game Feller, with his heart jumping and more than a little nervous, listened on the mound as the Indians manager Steve O'Neill (who was catching him that day) gave him some advice.

"Bob, don't fool with any curveballs," O'Neill said. "Just show Dizzy Dean, who is pitching for the Cardinals, what a fastball is really like!"

Feller took a peek into the Cardinals dugout where Ol' Diz, who just two years before had won 30 games, was sitting

Dean family collection, courtesy of Gene Kirby

Dizzy Dean reserved his praise for players he respected most. Cleveland right-hander Bob Feller certainly qualified.

and just staring into space. Feller pitched three innings and struck out eight of the nine batters he faced. Right after he finished, a photographer grabbed him before he could go into the clubhouse and took him over to the Cardinals dugout to meet Dizzy.

"Diz, how about taking a picture with this kid?" the photographer asked after spotting Dean.

Dizzy's answer never was forgotten by Feller.

"Podnah, if it's all right with him," Ol' Diz replied, "it's okay with me. After what he done thowed out there today, he's the one to say."

Dizzy knew a talent when he saw one.

"Fellow," Dizzy said as he held out his hand to Feller, "y'all sure thowed the hell outta that ball. Ya looked a lot like Ol' Diz!"

The young Bob Feller was genuinely moved by the compliment.

"Praise from Dizzy Dean," Feller said years later, "was something I've never forgotten."

Dizzy Dean always had time for kids and the working man. Here he poses with city workers, but Dizzy delighted in sticking his employers with the tab.

Dean family collection, courtesy of Gene Kirby

One notable exchange of correspondence typifies some of Dizzy Dean's antics on the road before he became a regular with the Cardinals. In a letter to the manager of the Houston Buffaloes, dated July 30, 1931, hotel manager J.E. Ellis of Charleston, Missouri, wrote:

"Dear Sir: We are writing to you in regards to the account which Dizzy Dean owes us from last winter when he spent the winter here. It amounts to $6.26. We have made several attempts to collect this from Dizzy, but he just ignores it.

"Mr. Bob Burroughs (hotel owner) asked us to write you about it. He said that you would see that the bill was paid. We would be very much obliged if you would attend to this at once for us." Signed, J.E. Ellis.

Houston Buffs president Fred Ankeman responded on Aug. 10, 1931, with this letter:

"Dear Sir (Mr. Ellis): We have your letter of July 30 advising us of the balance of $6.26 due you by Dizzy Dean. This boy manages to stay ahead of his salary and owing to his having just recently married and on account of other debts which have accumulated, he is having a hard time getting caught up.

At the present time it looks like the Houston club might get into the Dixie Series, and, if so, the Houston players will get several hundred dollars of extra money. If this thing materializes, I will make arrangements to take this money out and send it to you. If we cannot get it this way, I will try to arrange it some other way. In other words, you might have to wait a little while longer, but I think we can get this money to you sometime before the middle of September."

"Very truly yours (signed), Fred N. Ankenman, President.

Dizzy Dean was so proud of his younger brother Paul that he could hardly contain his enthusiasm. During the 1934 World Series, he didn't even try.

OL' DIZ AND GRANTLAND RICE

Dizzy asked the great sportswriter Grantland Rice prior to the first game of the 1934 World Series if Rice would mind talking to St. Louis manager Frankie Frisch about letting him pitch the entire series against the Detroit Tigers.

"Dizzy, you can't win four straight games!" said the sportswriter.

"I know that, Granny," Dean responded, "but I sure as shootin' can win four out of five."

Turns out, the big right-hander won only two games in the series, and his brother Paul won the other two. At least they kept it in the family!

DIZZY'S TOUR WITH A SATCHEL (PAIGE, THAT IS!)

★

When baseball was rising rapidly, exhibition games were commonly used to promote teams and players to a new and growing audience. One of the most profitable baseball barnstorming tours ever undertaken featured Dizzy Dean and his Major League All Stars against Leroy "Satchel" Paige and his Kansas City Monarchs.

Playing in big league ballparks shortly after the World Series ended from 1934-36, spill-over crowds of up to 35,000-40,000 were the norm. Dean and Paige were the main attractions.

It was agreed that they would pitch the first three innings of every game. Their fastballs popping into the big catchers mitts could be heard all over the ballparks, and the crowds loved it!

Ray Doan, a baseball promoter out of Hot Springs, Arkansas, who put together these tours, said being around Dizzy and Satch was like being a kid at a circus. You never knew what they were going to do... even to the extent that Satchel might not even show up for a game!

Dizzy told the story of one game when he was the leadoff hitter and hit a triple off Paige. "Running those bases I 'slud' into third base and was so tired I jest sat on the bag to catch my breath," Dean related. "I looked up and see Satchel comin' toward me."

The great Satchel Paige had words for Dean.

"Dizzy, don't you bother getting up," Satchel told him. "Just set there. You ain't goin' no futher."

"And I didn't," Dean recalled. "He struck out the next three batters!"

Those barnstorming tours, of course, were before the days of television when seeing Major League Baseball players in person away from the ballparks was still a novelty outside the National and American League cities. The West Coast cities had not been tapped. Dizzy made a lot of money out of these tours, and it was ironic that the first network televised Major League games to areas other than big league markets had as its star attraction Dizzy Dean.

Ray Doan may not have realized it at the time, but he firmly believed that it was Dizzy Dean to some extent who ultimately helped pave the way for the integration of the Major Leagues in 1947 with the debut of Jackie Robinson. Touring the country from coast to coast and the tremendous crowds that they drew opened the eyes of every Major League team owner and their baseball scouts to the caliber of play of black baseball stars. The fact that they held their own with white players, even though these were just exhibition games, convinced the owners that black players could compete in the bigs.

"Some of the big league owners," Doan said later, "didn't like it, and they let us know about it in no uncertain terms. It got to the point that I had to go before the Commissioner, Judge K.M. Landis, and get his approval for these barnstorming tours with the Kansas City Monarchs. The Judge had no objections. Branch Rickey, the vice president of the St. Louis Cardinals at the time, saw the future possibilities."

Years later, as general manager of the Brooklyn Dodgers, Rickey was the first to sign a black player (Robinson) to a Major League contract.

In the mid-1930s, three of the most highly acclaimed ballplayers of the decade talk shop. Left to right are Cecil Travis, Dizzy Dean and Satchel Paige, a legend of Negro Leagues fame with the Kansas City Monarchs.

Dean, along with Paige, treated everyone alike. On the ball field it was talent that mattered – not the color of a person's skin. This is not to say there was no prejudice shown at hotels and restaurants around the country. Problems developed in the matters of transportation, eating arrangements and such. Don't forget this was the 1930s.

The teams traveled in two buses. Satch and Dizzy traveled with them, but not with the other players. Together, they rode in Paige's Cadillac!

Imagine … In the days of sometimes-violent race relations and integration measures such as Brown v. Board of Education (1954), Dean and Paige leading an entourage of cars, trains or buses riding in one of their personal Cadillacs … Think of the looks when they stepped out of the same car in Birmingham, Mobile, New Orleans, Chattanooga, or dozens of towns where they played.

It wasn't long before these games outgrew minor league ballparks and were being played in places like Yankee Stadium, Griffith Stadium, Forbes Field, and Wrigley Field to near-capacity crowds. In New York they outdrew a Giants professional football game being played across the river in the Polo Grounds at the same time. In Griffith Stadium in Washington, Clark Griffith, the Senators owner, thought so little of the game when he first booked it that he insisted on only a flat guarantee of 10 percent of the gate. When "Griff" saw the full house in the park, he asked Dizzy and Satchel if they would mind raising his price – they did!

Paige, the hero of the defunct but historic Negro Leagues from 1924-47 and famed for his blazing fastball and just-as-quick wit, was accustomed to making headlines along with Dean wherever they traveled. Legend has it the rubber-armed Paige took the mound as a starter 29 times in 30 days for a predominantly white semi-pro squad in North Dakota.

Between grueling seasons with long drives and less-than-ideal housing conditions (mainly staying in black boarding homes or with friends or families in several cities due to racial inequity or lack of finances), Paige was able to negotiate appearance charges of anywhere from $300-$2,000 to take care of his personal expenses and meals. He often split his take with barnstorming teammates. His teams even traveled to Mexico, South America and the Caribbean when opposing teams and the money were prominent.

These Dean and Paige trips also gave fans a chance to see Paige matched against the likes of Joe DiMaggio, Stan Musial, Mickey Cochrane, Jimmie Foxx and other stars of the day as they watched the two prime performers pitch against one another.

"Paige was the best I've ever faced, and the fastest," DiMaggio said after one fruitless afternoon at the plate.

After the 1934 and '35 seasons (when Dean combined to pitch 54 games for the Cardinals), Paige and Dean went head-to-head six times with Paige winning four of those.

"My fastball looks like a change of pace alongside that pistol bullet old Satch shoots up to the plate," Dean said. "If Satch and I were pitching on the same team, we'd clinch the pennant by the Fourth of July and go fishing until World Series time."

Dean and such barnstorming groups as Bob Feller's All-Stars saw every one of the great black right-hander's arsenal of nine pitches, including the famed "hesitation" pitch (probably ruled a balk today) when Paige stopped in mid-delivery and then whipped a fastball at an unsuspecting hitter.

One year in the final game of their tour in Los Angeles, Dean and Paige really went at each other. They both pitched brilliantly for nine innings before leaving the mound. One Los Angeles writer said it was the best pitching duel he had ever seen. Wally Berger of the Braves, playing with Dean's All Stars, won the game with a home run. But they had to play 10 innings to decide this one.

Already in his mid-40s and past his physical prime, Paige pitched formally in the majors for most of five seasons (1948-52). With the 1948 Cleveland Indians, Satchel made a World Series appearance, but he is best remembered for his longevity.

So good for so long, Satchel pitched an amazing three shutout innings in 1965 for the Kansas City Athletics against Boston. Satch was 59 years old.

THE FATEFUL 1937 ALL-STAR GAME

★

In 1937 Dizzy was voted to the National League team in the All-Star Game. He didn't want to go to Washington, but his wife, Patricia, insisted he go. Pitching in the third inning, he was struck by a line drive off the bat of Earl Averill of the Cleveland Indians. The smash hit him on the big toe of his left foot, and he was immediately taken to the clubhouse.

A doctor was called in, and he examined Dean's toe.

"I've got bad news for you, Dizzy,"

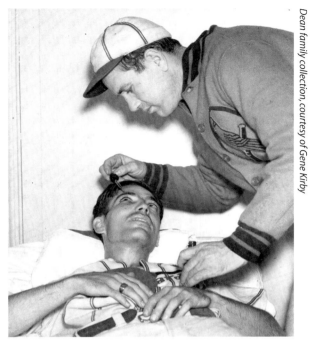

Dizzy Dean mugs for the camera as he pretends to tend to injured Cardinals teammate Don Gutteridge in 1936. During the All-Star Game the next year, it was Dizzy who required medical attention.

said the doctor, "that toe is fractured."

Dean looked up at him and said, "Hell, Doc, that toe ain't FRACA-TERD (fractured)!

"That toe is *broke*!"

(Left) Testosterone spewing all over the diamond, bench jockeying led to a Dizzy Dean-Tex Carlton dust-up in St. Louis between the Cubs and Cardinals that umpire George Barr tried to officiate. Today, the players are less likely to fight than their lawyers and agents.

BENCH JOCKEYING

If bench jockeys from the visiting club got on Dizzy Dean while he was pitching, he would just stop in the middle of his windup, bend over and look into the dugout to see who was yelling at him.

When Dizzy started taking notice, players on the bench would holler to their teammates to knock it off. They knew if they didn't shut up, Dizzy would bring them a present – special delivery.

Dean would start humming pitches right under the chin. "Just," Dizzy would chuckle, "to let them know I was out there!"

Dizzy Dean loved most everything associated with baseball, especially batting practice, as shown in this 1934 photo. He was, however, no fan of team meetings.

SKIP THE CLUBHOUSE MEETINGS

Dizzy Dean told me one time that after his first clubhouse meeting, it seems manager Frankie Frisch, a strong-willed personality in his own right, told Dizzy how to pitch to a certain hitter. Or tried to.

"I'm the greatest pitcher in baseball," Dean said, interrupting Frisch in front of the whole ballclub. "What's an infielder like you telling me how to pitch!"

That's how Dizzy's first pre-game meeting became his last.

SPELLING WASN'T DIZZY'S FORTE

Once Dean was signing an autograph before a game for a young lady. When the youngster told Dizzy her name was Helen, he asked if that was with one "l" or two.

DUCK SOUP AND DIZZY

One time I asked Dizzy Dean if all those close ballgames he pitched ever made him nervous or edgy. Did he ever get upset?

"Naw," the legend replied, "pitchin' in a close ballgame is 'duck soup' for me. I didn't even mind the big crowds when we wuz away from home.

"I had more to worry about when I was pitchin' ball in my bare feet out in the cow pasture!"

TOP SPORTS FIGURE OF 1934

(This news account came across the Associated Press wires nationwide on Dec. 19, 1934:)

(AP) NEW YORK, Dec. 19, 1934—Dizzy Dean, premier pitcher for the World Champion baseball team, rules the sporting roost of 1934 as the outstanding performer in any sport by virtually a landslide vote of acclaim in the fourth annual Associated Press sports poll.

Nearly 75 per cent of the ballots named him No. 1 athlete, amateur or professional. Lawson Little Jr., golfer of California, was second; Max Baer, pugilist of California, third; Fred Perry, Englishman and winner of the American singles tennis championship, fourth; Glen Cunningham, mile runner of Kansas, fifth.

Carl Hubbell, first strong pitcher of the New York National League baseball team, who was first place last year, failed to get a single vote in '34.

Seldom would you find a microphone, Dizzy Dean and humility in the same place, at the same time. His acceptance speech into the Hall of Fame was an exception. So, too, was his gracious impromptu speech when handed the 1934 Most Valuable Player award in 1935 Sportsman's Park in St. Louis. Dizzy was voted the '34 Sports Figure of the Year by the Associated Press.

Dean family collection, courtesy of Gene Kirby

In stark contrast to today, players from both World Series teams would pose for photos before and between games. Here in 1934, Dizzy Dean (left to right) and his manager Frank Frisch stand with Babe Ruth, Detroit's Mickey Cochrane and a distracted Schoolboy Rowe.

courtesy of the National Baseball Hall of Fame, Cooperstown, New York

His head in the game, Dizzy Dean caught a line drive on the noggin during the 1934 World Series. Cardinals teammates hauled him to the clubhouse. Dean recovered to beat the Detroit Tigers in a crucial Game 7.

In a spoof prior to Game 4 of the 1934 World Series in St. Louis, Dizzy Dean receives a World War I helmet from Detroit rival Billy Rogell. Earlier, Dizzy was just that, when Rogell presented him with a line drive to the skull.

Jubilant in the clubhouse, the Cardinals gather around their star pitchers, Dizzy Dean and, to his left, brother Paul Dean.

Family reunions can be held most anywhere most any time. Here, the Dean family gathers in St. Louis during the 1934 World Series. From left are A.M. "Ab" Dean, Elmer Dean, Dizzy Dean's wife Pat, Dizzy, Dorothy and Paul Dean.

Fresh off the World Series title in 1934, Dizzy Dean enjoys watching a spring training swing of aging Babe Ruth, who had been traded from the Yankees to the Boston Braves.

To the victor go the spoils. At left Paul Dean examines a toy tiger while Dizzy and Pat Dean soak up the adoration of Cardinals fans in their return to St. Louis after defeating the Detroit Tigers in the 1934 World Series.

In a pre-game ceremony at the old Baker Bowl in Philadelphia, Dizzy Dean towers over National League President Ford Frick and Phillies Manager Jimmy Wilson.

Competing on the base paths as well as the pitcher's mound, Dizzy Dean in 1936 slides safely into third base ahead of the tag by Chicago Cubs infielder Stan Hack.

Stars align in spring training. This 1937 shot captures legendary Yankee Joe DiMaggio with Dizzy Dean, whose careers were veering in opposite directions. DiMaggio is about to make the All-Star team for the second of 13 times, marry actress Dorothy Arnold and then in 1954 elope with glamorous movie star Marilyn Monroe. Dizzy was lucky in love, too, but the arm-weary pitcher is soon to be traded to the Chicago Cubs as damaged goods.

Dean family collection, courtesy of Gene Kirby

Sports writers of the day camped in Dizzy Dean's orbit, just waiting for the next quip. Chicago Times writer Irv Kupcinet is working on his next column.

Having been swapped to the Cubs, Dizzy Dean gives pointers during spring training in 1938 on Catalina Island, California.

Dean family collection, courtesy of Gene Kirby

Sobered by arm troubles and the resulting mediocre performance, Dizzy Dean in 1938 awaits his next start at Wrigley Field.

Dean family collection, courtesy of Gene Kirby

A despondent Dizzy Dean, just removed from a game at Wrigley Field, was not accustomed to failure.

Even on the downside of his career, Dizzy Dean could clown for the camera. This 1939 shot was taken in the Cubs clubhouse.

In 1939, despite declining mound performance, Dizzy Dean was still in demand for public appearances. For Cliff Maid bread, Dizzy was still, ahem, toast of the town.

Cubs pitchers Woody English and Charley Root flank legendary teammate Dizzy Dean. Was Dizzy giving tips on throwing the fastball? Or golf? Maybe betting the ponies or quail hunting?

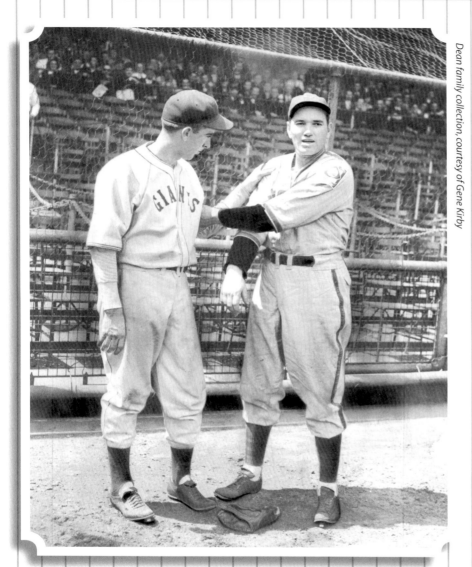

Dizzy Dean, his arm going dead from years of service, compares notes in the old Polo Grounds of New York with Giants Hall of Famer Carl Hubbell.

In 1940, nearing the end of a remarkable playing career, Dizzy Dean pals with brother Paul and cools off after another poor outing for the Cubs.

Once the ruler of this place, the retired Dizzy Dean steps on the mound at Sportsman's Park in St. Louis. By 1953, when this image was taken, Dizzy's broadcast career was blossoming.

For one of the few times in his life, the camera catches Dizzy Dean in somber reflection. In this 1941 shot, he has just been released by the Chicago Cubs.

Carrying joy in his heart and too much weight, Dizzy Dean pitches around his middle-aged spread in a 1959 Old-Timers Game at Yankee Stadium in New York.

Part IV

Man at the Mike

LIVING LARGE TO THE VERY LAST

"Dizzy just being Dizzy." It's an expression his producer and partner-in-fun Gene Kirby often used when trying to describe the old right-hander's behavior. Whether it was signing baseballs for a bunch of Dizzy Dean League youngsters or yucking it up with Mickey Mantle, Bob Hope and Tommy Dorsey at Prestonwood Country Club in Dallas, Dizzy Dean loved the limelight and relished being around people. He was nothing if not human, to the very core.

Beloved as he was by millions of doting fans, it is widely chronicled that when it came to broadcast agreements, real estate or use of his name, Dizzy, flanked by his ever-present wife, Pat, could turn stubborn as an Arkansas mule. And with Pat always nearby and keeping an eagle eye on contracts and expenses, Dean became an astute businessman and negotiator. Pat left him no other choice.

The Dizzy Dean persona that millions grew to know and love had its share of enemies. Friction that arose, often as not, was of Dizzy's making.

By the early 1960s, Pee Wee Reese (left) and Dizzy Dean were nearly as big as baseball itself, thanks to CBS Game of the Week every Saturday, sponsored by Falstaff Brewing. Producer Gene Kirby, himself a respected announcer of football and baseball, holds the cue cards for this commercial spot.

Mutual Radio's Al Helfer (Dean often called him Al *Heifer*) worked together, but outside the booth, their sizable egos often clashed and they eventually split, with hard feelings. Even the ultra-professional Buddy Blattner was later wounded in a Dean power play that pushed Dizzy's first broadcast partner out of the booth. The deliberate force-out paved the way to the rise of Pee Wee Reese at CBS as the only play-by-play TV announcer carried *nationwide*. Blattner and Dean later reconciled when Blattner took the high road, inviting Dizzy to share some innings in a Kansas City Royals' broadcast in the early 1970s.

For years, network executives winced and wrung their hands when Dizzy would deliberately flout a major advertiser or intentionally butcher the names of players. Worse, Dizzy was found to be ill-prepared and steadfastly unprofessional – even disloyal, ham-handed and petty at a personal level. For her part, Pat was variously described as everything from supportive to pushy, depending on which side of the Dean interests you took.

The New York media establishment, flexing new-found muscle from television revenues, grew weary of what one network exec called "country corn" and "barnyard bromides." Dean biographer Curt Smith quoted CBS Sports Director Bill MacPhail as both lavishly praising Dizzy – and ripping him to ribbons.

"In the hinterlands it was incredible," MacPhail says of ratings. "Watching Dizzy Dean was a religion. An absolute religion … He was the first announcer *ever* to inject comedy into a game."

But, on the flip side: "We had no control over what he might say. We would sit in front of our TV sets and cringe … I didn't care for him personally … He was much warmer, in fact, on the air … I wouldn't say he was just a big hillbilly, because he could be very cunning. Not my kind of person. Very hard to handle."

Eventually, the feeling became mutual, creating a long-festering sore in the mid-1960s that led to a final break-up. Looking back, most agree, the big losers were baseball and baseball fans. – *Bo Carter*

PRODUCTION MEETINGS AND COMPUTER BASEBALL
★

Before every Game of the Week telecast a meeting was held to go over the production aspects of the upcoming game with the talent, network producers and agency representatives. Out of deference to Dizzy, these meetings were held in his hotel room because he invariably would attend dressed in his uniform of the day, his pajamas.

CBS Sports one season had made an arrangement with a computer company based in Phoenix, Arizona, to supply statistical data to be used on our ball games. This included the averages of hitters with runners in scoring position at third base and second base, with or two outs, or with the score tied or trailing by one run, etc. When these situations came up, the information would be punched up

and shown on the monitor in the booth. The announcers would be expected to comment on it and to tell our viewers what those numbers meant.

Dean always looked upon any new gimmick with suspicion, especially if it was a recommendation of the network. Ol' Diz just wanted to do things the way

Baseball, television - life in general - was once much simpler. Even then, Dizzy Dean didn't much care for production meetings. In these 1956 shots from old Connie Mack Stadium in Philadelphia, spliced together by Gene Kirby, Dizzy and Gene play gin rummy. In his notes, Gene admits they were supposed to be prepping for a Falstaff commercial.

he always had. If he had been doing things a certain way all these years, why change? Before talking to Diz about the new computer idea, the agency held a meeting of its own with the CBS production group.

CBS was told it might be a problem getting Dean involved in this idea. The agency felt sure he would not cooperate and would in their opinion raise one helluva stink. CBS personnel said they had a lot of money tied up with the computer company and that the package extended beyond using it only on the Game of the Week. They insisted the agency make every effort to see that Dizzy went along with the idea.

The night before one game at a meeting in the Roosevelt Hotel in New York, a CBS producer and the computer representative explained to everyone present how the computer worked and how it should be handled with the viewing audience. Dizzy listened very attentively and agreed with everything being said. "Podnahs," he said, "it sounds great. I unnerstand everything perfectly, and I'll be glad to work with y'all!"

The agency people were flabbergasted! They couldn't believe what they had just heard. Ol' Diz had to be sick. He couldn't be feeling well. Was this the same agitating, haggling, disruptive Dean who constantly fought everything that wasn't standard operating procedure? The meeting lasted 10 minutes.

CBS officials, pleased with the results, left the room with the impression that the agency just didn't know how to handle Dizzy. No problems. It was all very simple. Tell him what they wanted to do, and that was it!

The boys from CBS had hardly gotten out of the door when Dean turned to everyone. "Podnahs, now let's get something straight," he said. "They ain't no way Ol' Diz is gonna do anything like they want me to do. They can take this computer (bleep) and stick it up their asses! I don't even unnerstand what the hell they wuz talkin' about. So how in hell am I gonna explain something to the fans that I don't know nuthin' about? Anyway, I'm in the booth to broadcast a baseball game … not those damn COMMUTERS (computers)!"

"But Dizzy," one of the agency people said, "just a few minutes ago you told those fellows from CBS and the computer company that you understood perfectly everything they were saying and you would be happy to work with them and that it was a great idea. If you didn't want any part of it, why the hell didn't you say so? You could have told them to forget it."

"I just didn't feel like sittin' around with them doggone guys from CBS any longer than I had to," Dean answered. "The way I look at it is when I get to the ballpark tomorrow and they find that I ain't gonna do what they want me to do, it'll just agitate the living (bleep) out of them! I was gettin' hongry and figured we oughtn't waste any more time before we all went out to eat and have a couple of 'cold ones.'" End of meeting …

During the game the next day the computer information was fed into the monitors in the broadcast booth and Dean completely ignored it. The information was punched up again and still no comment from Dizzy. The CBS producer called on the intercom and wanted Dean to talk about the computer numbers. Dean blew his stack right on the air! "Folks," he shouted, "you seen them numbers on your cameries (TV sets)! I don't know nuthin' about them, and couldn't care less! I guarantee one thing: Ol' Diz ain't gonna try to explain somethin' to y'all that I don't know nuthin' about! And, futhermore, as far as I'm concerned, it ain't got a doggone thing to do with what's goin' on in the ball game. I'm here to talk baseball, not a bunch of STATICS (statistics)!" CBS was fit to be tied.

★ RADIO TICKERS

In the late 1930s and 1940s, only the home baseball games were broadcast on radio live. The announcers did not travel on the road with the clubs. Instead, they would go to the radio studio and recreate the game via the Western Union ticker.

This, of course, gave the announcers a great deal of leeway as far as filling in with their own comments on the games. This was right up Ol' Diz's alley, and he played it to the hilt. He was the only baseball announcer I ever knew who drew an audience to the studio to watch him recreate a ballgame over a ticker.

One day during a key Brooklyn-St. Louis game that was coming in over the ticker, an erudite individual working the wire came in with the following message: "The Cardinals have loaded the bases with nobody out. It could be catastrophic for the Dodgers." The tape was handed to Dean.

"CA-TAS-TOFIC (catastrophic)," he blurted, "is he the new pitcher for the Dodgers?"

When the inning had ended and the situation was explained to Dizzy, he was aggravated. "Why didn't that feller jest say the Dodgers wuz in a bad spot, iffen that's what he meant?" Dean snapped.

Dean family collection, courtesy of Gene Kirby

Historians say the St. Louis Cardinals first experimented with radio broadcasting in 1926, granting Midwest powerhouse KMOX the rights to cover a partial schedule of home games. This 1941 shot shows Dizzy Dean working a Browns-Cards game. In years before, early broadcasters were not actually on-site, but depicted game action from Western Union tickers – which gave the likes of Dizzy huge license to improvise.

Once Dizzy Dean and Pee Wee Reese got comfortable working together on CBS Game of the Week broadcasts, they converted their playful off-camera behavior to massive popularity on camera.

THE POST-TELECAST ROUTINE

After every telecast Dizzy, Pee Wee and I would go back to the hotel to clean up before going out to dinner. We'd sit around and BS a little bit, and Dizzy would often call his wife Patricia to get her opinion about how the broadcast had come off when she didn't travel with him.

The conversation usually went something like this:

"Hi, Mom?" Dean would begin. "How ya doin'? Did ya see the ballgame? Uh, huh … well, I thought you seen it. How'd I do, Mom? Uh, huh … ya thought I done great. Well, I thought so, too, Mom. I jest can't he'p it, ya know. How was Pee Wee, Mom (a long pause while Dizzy listened)? Yeah, I'll tell him, Mom. Yeah, he's right here. Naw, don't you worry none. He won't be upset 'cause he knows you always tell the truth. Yeah, I'll tell him, Mom. See ya tomorrow night. I love ya, too; bye now."

Then Dean put down the telephone.

"What did Patricia have to say, Dizzy?" Pee Wee asked.

"Well, naturally, she thought I done a helluva job!" Ol' Diz said with a big grin.

"Of course," Pee Wee added, "what did you think she'd say? What did she have to say about me?"

"Pat thought you were horseshit!" Dizzy exclaimed.

"Now, that's funny, Diz," Pee Wee replied. "I called my wife Dotty just before I came up here, and she said the same thing about you, only Dotty didn't use the same word Patricia did!"

NOBLE PRONUNCIATION

While broadcasting a Reds-Giants game on radio, Dizzy called the New York catcher Ray Noble. Noble, coming from Havana and being Hispanic, actually pronounced his name "NO-blay." Every announcer called him "NO-blay" … except Dean.

Listening to the broadcast in Florida

Dean family collection, courtesy of Gene Kirby

that day was Ol' Diz's former teammate Pepper Martin. About half an hour later, a telegram arrived in the booth for Dean.

It read:

"Jerome, If you insist calling NO-blay Noble, how would you pronounce CAFÉ? Signed, Johnny Leonard Martin (Martin's real name).

Dizzy read the wire on the air and told the audience, "Why, Pepper, I'd call that a RESTAURANT!"

By the mid-1950s, when this image of Dizzy Dean and Gene Kirby was taken before a game in Philadelphia, Diz was already catching good-natured ribbing from his former Cardinal teammates.

Dean family collection, courtesy of Falstaff Brewing and Gene Kirby

FALSTAFF'S FINEST

Anyone who ever listened to a Dizzy Dean broadcast knew that he worked for the Falstaff Brewing Corp. of St. Louis. When he first came to the brewery, Falstaff was selling approximately 600,000 barrels of beer a year. Twenty years later, they were selling about 2 million barrels per year, and Falstaff had bought breweries in San Jose, California, Fort Wayne, Indiana and Galveston, Texas.

Years ago, Dean was the principal speaker at a brewer's convention in St. Louis. Most of the owners and the top

Once sponsors discovered Dizzy Dean's popularity with the viewing audience, they gave the old right-hander more freedom at the mike. Friends say Diz would have taken liberties in any case.

82 Part IV | Man at the Mike

brass of the major breweries were there: Gussie Busch of Budweiser, Joe and Buddy Griesedieck and Harvey Beffa of Falstaff, Fred Miller of Miller's, and others from Schlitz, Pabst, Rheingold, etc.

Never one to toot his own horn except when he got up to speak, which was quite often, Ol' Diz took credit for the tremendous sales of Falstaff beer. Rightfully so, he said more than once. He closed out his talk by saying, "And, gentlemen, let me tell you one more thing. When the people at Falstaff want more beer, they go out and buy more breweries. When the people at Budweiser want more beer, they go out and buy more horses!"

The first person out of his chair was Gussie Busch of Budweiser, laughing all the way as he rushed over to shake Dean's hand!

Dizzy Dean interviews a wary Yogi Berra in the 1960s at old Yankees Stadium. The Yankees legend knows that at any moment, he could become the butt of a Dizzy joke.

RUSS "MONK" MEYER

During a telecast one afternoon, Dizzy and Pee Wee Reese began talking about Russ Meyer, the former Major League pitcher known as "The Mad Monk." Russ had spent three years-plus with the Dodgers in Brooklyn with Pee Wee.

After Meyer retired from baseball, he became the owner of a 40-lane bowling alley in Aurora, Illinois. Pee Wee gave Dizzy all that information about the new facility.

"Podnah," Ol' Diz noted, "I'll bet some of them there bowlers is throwin' more strikes in his bowlin' alley than Russ did when he was pitchin'!"

Dean family collection, courtesy of Falstaff Brewing and Gene Kirby

Dean family collection, courtesy of Falstaff Brewing and Gene Kirby

Dizzy was never shy about expressing his opinions, but Diz left managing a team to the likes of Baltimore skipper Paul Richards.

"How would you like to manage the Cubs?" he asked Dean. "Podnah," Ol' Diz replied without hesitation, "I might be Dizzy ... but I ain't crazy!"

DIZZY'S THOUGHTS ABOUT MANAGING THE CUBBIES

★

Flying into Chicago one day for a game at Wrigley Field, Dizzy and I met sportswriter Jimmy Enright, who rode in a taxi with us to the ballpark. The Cubs were not having one of their better years. As a matter of fact, they hadn't been doing so well for quite a few years.

At one point in the conversation about baseball, Enright turned to Dizzy.

DIZZY AND DALE MITCHELL

★

During a game in Cleveland, outfielder Dale Mitchell came up to hit. "Here's the ol' left-handed hitter hisself comin' to the plate for the second time," Dizzy said. "As I told you folks LATER today (Ol' Diz obviously meant earlier), Dale has hit in 16 straight games."

Mitchell proved Dean prophetic when he later hit safely to extend the streak.

Dean family collection, courtesy of Gene Kirby

Master of the ad lib, Dizzy Dean was also lucky when it came to covering his mistakes. Here Diz interviews noted pro golfer Mike Souchak at a Houston event in the 1950s.

CRITIC OF THE MAN

Some fan in the Midwest, not exactly enamored with Dizzy's broadcasting of baseball games, wrote to his local newspaper. "I think Dizzy Dean is as funny as a Kansas tornado and contains as much wind," the writer said. "But at least a tornado blows itself out!"

SIMULCASTING

Dizzy for many years had broadcast baseball on radio and TV, but he never had done a simulcast – that's radio and television at the same time. Trying to explain to his audience how this was done, he said, "Folks, Ol' Diz is sure havin' a tough time with this. It's like talking outta both sides of my mouth at the same time.

Dean family collection, courtesy of Gene Kirby

The technical side of sports broadcasting was lost on Dizzy Dean, but his humor and homespun wisdom gained him an enormous national audience. Working the 1953 Hall of Fame game in Cooperstown, New York, the old right-hander is bearing down, with producer-friend Gene Kirby feeding him game notes.

"I don't wanna talk too much about what's goin' on," he continued, "'cause you people watchin' on television can see it. But you fans who's listenin' to the game over your radios will get mad 'cause if I don't talk about it, y'all won't know what's happenin' 'cause you can't see it!

"In this business they call it SIMUL-STANCE (simulcast)," he added. "To be honest with ya, I'd jest as soon be back home in Dallas!"

Once asked if he ever threw a spitball, Dizzy Dean told his interviewer that he never needed an illegal pitch. These two Dodger aces, Sandy Koufax and Don Drysdale, didn't need it either.

A "TYPICAL" NEWS CONFERENCE

Q. Dizzy, who was the toughest hitter you ever faced?

A. None of 'em gave Ol' Diz any trouble, Podnah. But the two guys I hated to see walkin' up to the plate wuz Paul and Lloyd Waner of the Pittsburgh Pirates. It seemed like every time I looked up, Lloyd was runnin' down to first base, and Paul was on his way to third. They wuz two good hitters!"

Q. Did Lew Burdette really throw a 'spitter?' (Burdette was a Major League pitcher for 18 years with six clubs, most of them with Milwaukee, and was always accused of throwing a spitball).

A. No, I don't think Lew did. It's all SOSS-KO-LOGIS-HAL (psychological). Now when the hitter sees a pitcher goin' through all them there motions, he starts thinkin' and that's when you got 'em! That's when they's finished. Them big thinkers ain't big hitters. That's my opinion.

Q. Did you ever throw a spitball?

A. No, Podnah (grinning). I never had to; I got them hitters out by just foggin' 'em in there with my fastball. Sometimes I'd even tell 'em what I was gonna thow and still got 'em out!"

Q. How does a hitter get out of a slump?

A. I'm glad you asked me that. Do you know what them hittin' coaches tell their hitters? They say don't try hittin' the ball to the left or right, jest right up the middle, and that burns me up! Who's standin' there right in the middle? The poor ol' pitcher!

"All I got is a li'l ol' ball in my hand, and he's got that big bat waving it back 'n forth. And I'm only 60 feet, six inches away from him. When I hit a batter everybody got upset. When the batter hit me with a line drive, I guess that wuz different. He wuz getting' out of his slump!"

FRACTURING THE ENGLISH LANGUAGE

Responding to the furor of his fracturing of the English language on his broadcasts by the schoolteachers in Missouri, Dean asked for relief.

"Them teachers don't like when I say Enos Slaughter or Stan MOO-SIAL (Musial) or Terry Moore slud into second base," he noted. "What do they want me to say – slidded?"

"Back when me and my brother Paul wuz pitchin' for the Cardinals Gas House Gang," he continued, "I'd win a game, and then Paul would win the next one. Nobody come around the clubhouse and asked us did we 'thowed' or 'throwed' our fastball over the plate to get the batter out.

"I don't even know Webster's front name," he concluded, "but how many of them teachers ever give a talk at Harvard

Dean family collection, courtesy of Gene Kirby

English teachers would cringe when they heard Dizzy Dean butcher the language, but he connected with a vast audience. In the 1950s, Dizzy's wife, Pat, was enlisted to gather fan mail.

University, like me? I give a talk on 'Announcin' I Have Did!' I also got a laugh outta them when I started my talk by sayin' 'Ladies and Gentleman ... ' How's I to know that they didn't allow no girls into Harvard at that time?"

PEE WEE'S BIG ARGUMENT

Dizzy and Pee Wee Reese were broadcasting a game in Cincinnati, and the question about arguing with umpires came up. Pee Wee told of the time he got involved with umpire Lee Ballanfant about a strike call.

"I gave Ballanfant a little too much conversation," Pee Wee remembered, "and he told me it was going to cost me 25 bucks if I didn't stop. Well, I didn't stop and I told him to go ahead and make it 50 bucks! I didn't care!"

Dizzy couldn't believe what he was hearing from the normally mild-mannered Reese.

"Gosh, Podnah, I never said nuthin' like that to no umpire in my life," Dean told Pee Wee. "After all, I worked for Mr. Branch Rickey, who wuz general manager with the Cardinals when I wuz

As a player, Pee Wee Reese was mild-mannered, but an umpire's ruling could get him irritated. But baseball was an afterthought during this 1961 dinner in the Hawaiian Room of the old Hotel Lexington in New York. Left to right are Gene Kirby, an unidentified couple, Pat Dean, Pee Wee Reese and Dizzy Dean.

in St. Louis, and I couldn't afford to say nuthin' like that there. Branch Rickey was well known for not payin' his players a lot of money."

Dizzy Dean claims he never threw at hitters with intent to injure, only to intimidate. His rivals of yesteryear disagreed. The Indians' Bobby Avila chuckles with Dean's broadcast partner Buddy Blattner in 1955 at Cleveland Municipal Stadium.

Despite Dizzy Dean's mood on this modest TV set in 1953, contract negotiations with Falstaff Brewing could get intense. Dizzy's wife, Pat - a generation ahead of most women in the workplace - would often intercede on behalf of her husband.

THROWING AT HITTERS

★

One time after a batter had been hit by a pitched ball, Pee Wee asked Dizzy if he ever threw at hitters. Pee Wee actually knew damn well that Dizzy did! Dean pretended to be offended.

"No, not to hurt 'em, Podnah," Dean said, "but I had to let 'em know I was out there! I never did like it when them hitters come up to the plate with their chewin' gum planted on top of the button on their caps. That's when I would thow a pitch right for that gum! Somethin' else I didn't like wuz when them fellers come out of the dugout swingin' two or three bats over their heads and lookin' too damn CONFIDENTIAL (confident)!"

ONLY DEAN COULD GET AWAY WITH THIS

★

In his sports broadcasting career, hardly anyone has been able to say the things on the air that Dizzy Dean would say about players, coaches, managers, and executives, and continue working in baseball. Questions that would have been embarrassing to ask were greeted with raucous laughter by those being questioned by Ol' Diz.

On a pre-game telecast between Cleveland and the Chicago White Sox, Dizzy was seated between the two general managers – Frank Lane of the White Sox

During interviews, Dizzy Dean loved to make baseball figures squirm with a ticklish question. Diz had plenty of targets during this 1961 dinner in Scottsdale, Arizona. Standing is Gene Kirby, with Lefty O'Doul and the legendary Ty Cobb.

"DIZZY" DEAN   GENE KIRBY   "LEFTY" O'DOUL   TY COBB

Both general managers roared with laughter! The question was never answered.

FALSTAFF'S PROMO

and Hank Greenberg of the Indians. Before introducing his guests, Dizzy had told the fans how easily he had handled Greenberg in the 1934 World Series between the Tigers and the Cardinals. Dean struck out Greenberg five times in three games with three of those strikeouts coming in the seventh and final game of the series.

"The only reason I'm sittin' between 'em is to stop 'em from pickin' each other's pockets," grinned Ol' Diz at one point in the pre-game broadcast.

"Now, Mr. Lane did you ever try to 'rook' Mr. Greenberg in a players' deal? What I mean is, did you ever try to sell him a player you knew was no good?"

One year the Falstaff Brewing Corp. was sponsoring football on television in addition to baseball. During a rehearsal of a commercial with Dizzy, it was agreed that when he mentioned baseball, I would toss him a baseball. When he mentioned football, I would throw him a football.

At the end of the inning of a baseball game, Dean was ready to go. When he said, "Falstaff not only brings you baseball … (my cue to toss him a baseball)" I threw the ball, and he caught it.

Ol' Diz then said, "And Falstaff also brings you football … (my cue to throw him a football)" I tossed the football, and he dropped it!

For the next 20 seconds all the camera picked up was the top of Dean's cowboy hat with him on his hands and knees talking and trying to pick up the football! When he came back up and sat down in his chair, he had the biggest grin on his face, but he was still talking and holding the football.

This is how he finished the Falstaff commercial:

"Folks, let me tell you once more. Whether you're at home watchin' the ballgame or in your favorite tavern, enjoy a good ol' bottle or can of Falstaff – the choicest product of the brewers art. It's America's premium quality BALL … er … I mean beer!"

In this 1955 CBS interview with Yankees shortstop Phil Rizzuto before an exhibition game with the Dodgers at old Ebbets Field in Brooklyn, Dizzy Dean appears to be on cue. Such was not always the case, as the brass at Falstaff Brewing could tell you.

His old producer, Gene Kirby, left, can vouch for the fact that Dizzy Dean didn't always follow the script. Here, Diz and CBS play-by-play man Pee Wee Reese rehearse a commercial for Falstaff Brewing. It is not known how many takes were required.

IT WAS MOTHER'S DAY

One Sunday afternoon while rehearsing a Falstaff commercial for the upcoming TV Game of the Week, Dizzy refused to pick up the bottle of Falstaff. I asked him why.

"Podnah, this is Mother's Day," he said. "How do you think all them mothers watching us out there today is gonna feel, if on their day Ol' Diz asks 'em to drink or go out and buy a bottle or can of beer?"

I told him there was nothing wrong with it. Many of those same mothers might be drinking a beer anyway. Furthermore, it was important to Falstaff, which was paying him a ton of money a year, that it would help sell more of its product if he did tell the mothers to pick up some Falstaff at their favorite grocery store or have a cold one at their favorite tavern or bar.

Dean was adamant. "I ain't gonna do it," he said. And he DIDN'T!

This agitated the living hell out of everybody at the brewery, the advertising agency and the network! But that was Ol' Diz!

JOHNNY PESKY GETS TOSSED

In 1952 Dizzy and I were doing a broadcast for Mutual's Game of the Day on radio. We were in Detroit in mid-August, and Johnny Pesky, a good friend who was traded to the Tigers from the Boston Red Sox in June, was the hitter. Johnny got into an argument in the first inning with the plate umpire, John Flaherty, and was thrown out of the game.

"Podnah, I can't understand it," I turned to Dizzy on the broadcast and said. "I never saw Johnny Pesky thrown out of a game before."

Ol' Diz looked over at me and with a

More than once, when Dizzy Dean was broadcasting a game, he needed the emergency bail-out of Gene Kirby, his play-by-play man for the old Mutual radio Game of the Day and later, his producer for CBS Game of the Week telecasts.

silly grin on his face said, "I understand why he got thowed (thrown) out. His wife jest got into Dee-troit this morning, and he ain't seen her since he was traded from Boston a couple of months ago."

"That's great," was all I could say. "Now let's get back to the ballgame!"

Dean family collection, courtesy of Gene Kirby

Frank Madson photo courtesy of the Wichita Beacon

For decades, the National Baseball Congress promoted youth baseball and sent many players to the pros and college ranks. In this 1952 photo, left to right, Gene Kirby, Pat and Dizzy Dean, George Sisler and Paul Dean are honored in a 1952 ceremony in Wichita, Kansas.

Immediately after retiring from baseball, Dizzy Dean in 1941 began a long and storied career in broadcasting. His first baseball play-by-play man, at station KWK in St. Louis, was Johnny O'Hara. Diz worked with O'Hara through 1944, then came back in '46 and '47. By '45, Harry Caray was working Cardinals games with Gabby Street. The St. Louis market also showcased Jack Buck, Joe Garagiola and Mike Shannon. Small wonder the Cards are firmly entrenched with fans in middle America.

Dizzy Dean and Gene Kirby ham it up while the retired Cardinals pitcher gets a 1954 haircut in Lancaster, Texas barber shop.

Quite a road crew. (Left to right) Dizzy Dean, Paul Jonas, Al Helfer and Gene Kirby pause before a 1953 Mutual radio broadcast from Payne Field, winter home of the Red Sox in Sarasota, Florida.

Play-by-play man Buddy Blattner, producer Gene Kirby and Dizzy Dean broadcast a 1955 Game of the Week for CBS TV. Blessed with tremendous hand-eye coordination, Blattner won the world men's doubles table tennis championship in 1936, played part of the 1942 season with the St. Louis Cardinals and following a World War II hitch in the Navy, played four more years with the Giants and Phillies.

An East Texas "howdy" greets the arrival of Gene Kirby, Pat and Dizzy Dean. This shot is believed to be of Pepper Martin's daughter, taken at the Tyler airport in 1955.

The world began to shrink, especially for pro sports, with the advent of commercial air travel. In 1955, Dizzy Dean and Gene Kirby pose with a flight attendant after a stop in Waterloo, Iowa. Both Braniff and what was then called a stewardess are now extinct.

Never ones to pass up a good time, the smiling Gene Kirby and Dizzy Dean stop for a local interview during the 1956 Hillbilly Festival in Meridian, Mississippi.

Former Cardinal Dizzy Dean and ex-New York Giant Carl Hubbell – once bitter pitching rivals – swap stories in 1956 at the old Polo Grounds in New York.

In demand far and wide, Dizzy Dean takes a healthy cut during a public appearance in Souix City, Iowa. In his prime, Dizzy called himself a "purdy fur country hitter."

Dizzy Dean was always looking for his next laugh. With Yogi Berra, in 1956 at old Ebbets Field in Brooklyn, he didn't have to wait long.

Whether it was back home in Lucas, Arkansas, pretending to pick cotton with Gene Kirby, or speaking to the Tennessee legislature in Nashville in 1957, Dizzy Dean was a man of ease and good will.

Dizzy Dean admired a skilled performer in any endeavor. In 1957, Diz was especially drawn to crafty Yankees left-hander Bobby Schantz, a gritty 5-7, 139-pounder who survived for 16 years in the majors without an overpowering fastball.

During the 1937 All-Star game, Dizzy Dean famously caught an Earl Averill line drive with his foot. Carried off the field, Dizzy later told a doctor, "Fractured! My toe is broke!" Before the 1963 All-Star game in Yankee Stadium, Averill and Dean relive the moment.

Dizzy Dean knew how to ride in style. His producer-sidekick Gene Kirby (middle) and Falstaff Brewing made sure their star color analyst made an impression.

Dean family collection, courtesy of Falstaff Brewing and Gene Kirby

Dean family collection, courtesy of Gene Kirby

The Yankees 1965 Old-Timers Day at Yankee Stadium brought out the legends. (1ˢᵗ row, left to right) Bill Terry, Giants; Joe DiMaggio, Yanks; Bill Dickey, Yanks; Dizzy Dean, Cards and Cubs. (back row, left to right) Gabby Hartnett, Cubs; Joe McCarthy, manager, Giants; Frank "Home Run" Baker, A's; Zach Wheat, Dodgers; Frank Frisch, Cards; Rogers Hornsby, Cards.

With Dizzy Dean around, a mike was never far away. Neither were (left to right) former Dodgers Junior Gilliam and Pee Wee Reese, along with ex-Cleveland legend Bob Feller, as they gathered for a public appearance in the mid-1960s.

Dean family collection, courtesy of Gene Kirby

Happy anglers Dizzy Dean and Gene Kirby caught this collection of fillets-to-be while fishing off the coast of Mississippi in 1966.

Of the many faces of Dizzy Dean, most were lit with joy. Has anybody had more fun "working" than Diz?

Part V

Diz & Pat

SO CLOSE FOR SO LONG

Details of the first meeting of Patricia Nash and Dizzy Dean in Houston in spring 1930 remain lost to time and the telling, even for Gene Kirby and other close friends. Gene noted that Dizzy did not confide many details of their courtship, but while Diz thought a wedding at home plate at Houston's Buffs Stadium might be a possibility, Pat was dead-set against any such publicity stunt.

Instead, she reserved the First Christian Church, near the Rice University campus. Her firm venue choice was a sign of things to come.

This all got started, baseball legend has it, just when Dizzy Dean was developing a dubious practice of running up debts on clothing and meals – leaving his employer stuck with the bill. One such spending spree in the spring of 1930 took the young right-hander into a Houston department store where Dizzy had spotted spiffy suits he could charge to the Buffs baseball club. Then, fate and pheromones intervened.

This 1931 wedding day photo of Dizzy Dean and his bride, Pat, shows a happy couple about to take life's journey together.

Dizzy happened to meet a store staffer named Patricia Nash, who would become a regular at Buffs' games for the rest of the long, hot summer of 1930. When Dizzy was relegated to start the 1931 season in minor league Houston – against his wishes – the love between the pitcher and Pat continued to blossom, culminating in plans for a June 15, 1931 wedding.

From Dizzy's view-point, home plate at Houston's Buff Stadium appeared as good a place as any to hold a wedding ceremony. His bride-to-be, however, made it abundantly clear that Dizzy's ceremonial first pitch was nowhere near the strike zone. Research has not yielded a wedding invitation nor a guest list, but a photo of the nuptials has been found. The ceremony, a generation before widespread use of air conditioning, must have been a hot summer highlight for Sweat City socialites. Her steadfast choice of First Christian Church was a sign of things to come. No way would her nuptials provide fodder for a Dizzy publicity stunt.

Pat would not only run the Dean household but, ahead of her time, haggle with baseball club execs over Dizzy's contracts – a fact that exasperated the likes of prideful Cardinals General Manager Branch Rickey. Indeed, the ever-present Pat was one of the few player's wives allowed to accompany her husband on team road trips, on the club's dime. "Pat," an old friend would chuckle some 50 years later, "definitely ruled the roost."

The Deans never had children. But beginning in 1931 until Dizzy was laid to rest in 1974 – whether it was fishing or lounging on the beach, dining with celebrity friends or cruising to Hawaii – just having each other proved to be plenty for both. – *Mark S. McDonald*

PATRICIA DEAN — DESERVING OF EQUAL TIME

★

Somewhere she waits to make you win
Your soul in her firm white hands;
Somewhere the gods have made for you
The woman who understands.

–Everard Jack Appleton (1872-1931)

Many years ago, Mrs. Dizzy Dean told a sports writer, "Getting the hitters out and winning ball games is Dizzy's business. I know how the money is to be made and what to do with it. Save it! That's my part of our relationship. A ballplayer isn't a star all his life, though some of them think it will last forever. They are the ones for whom I feel sorry. When the time comes for Dizzy to leave baseball, I want him to get out gracefully and with money in his pocket."

Patricia Dean upheld that part of her deal. When it came to doing business with Dizzy Dean, you dealt with his wife.

When he finished his career as a player and as a broadcaster, the Deans were independently wealthy.

Patricia Dean's entire married life with Dizzy – 43 years – was devoted to the care and feeding of her husband. If many saw her to be tough, it was because she had to be. When she felt someone was trying to take advantage of Dizzy, look out! When they married, Dizzy was like a young colt being turned loose in a corral for the first time. You had to rope him first, which she did. Then you had to smooth him down to get him to run quietly. Finally, he was made to realize that throwing his money away and then borrowing money without a thought of paying it back were things that responsible men just didn't do.

The important thing was to channel Dizzy Dean's boyish, some would say childish, enthusiasm and exuberance in the right direction without ever losing his "country" disposition and sense of humor. Pat did just that. The popping off that Dizzy did throughout his career got

him into countless scrapes and squabbles, both on and off the field. It never seemed to bother Ol' Diz very much.

He could, however, blow his top with the very best! But his lack of education was never a problem for Dizzy. "Podnah, I get a kick out of them there college fellahs always tryin' to tell me what to do," he told me many times. "Ya' know, they's all workin' like hell to make a livin', and here's me and Patricia 'livin' high on the uppermost part of the hog!' "

"If Dizzy had gotten an education," Patricia Dean often said, "there's no doubt in my mind, he could have been anything he wanted … even President of the United States." (Aw, come on, Pat!) Then with a snip of a smile on her face, she would add, "Perhaps if he'd been any smarter, then he might not have married me."

Dizzy told Patricia that he wanted them to be married at home plate at the Houston ballpark before a night game that he was scheduled to pitch. Diz had it all figured.

"We'll get married at the ballpark," he said, "and some of them fans will want to give a great pitcher like me some presents." Patricia put her foot down hard on that idea. She maintained that it was all right to kid around about some things – but not marriage.

Patricia Nash and Jay Hanna Dean were married at the First Christian Church in Houston, on June 15, 1931. He was a pitcher for the Houston Buffaloes of the Texas League. Patricia worked for

Strong-willed Patricia Nash Dean (right) not only was the only player's wife to travel to St. Louis road games with her husband, Dizzy Dean, on the team's dime, she negotiated Dizzy's contracts. Here she pauses prior to a 1935 round of golf with other player wives during the Cardinals' spring training in Bradenton, Florida.

Dean family collection, courtesy of Gene Kirby

Dizzy Dean gets help from wife Pat in carving up a toy tiger, symbolizing the Dean-led St. Louis Cardinals' 1934 World Series over the Detroit Tigers. More good times lie ahead.

a department store in town. Dizzy even had the date of their wedding screwed up for years. He often told people he was married on June 10 – that was five days before it actually took place.

"I always thought we wuz married the day we took out the weddin' license," he said. Dizzy booted another one on his wedding day. When taking their vows in answer to the question of taking this woman to be your lawful wedded wife, he replied, "I will, sir," instead of "I do." The minister also omitted the word obey. Here's guessing that he just figured it would be superfluous.

Dizzy gave the minister a "generous" $1.50 for performing the wedding service.

In spring 1935, Dizzy Dean was a holdout. After all, he had won 30 games and two more in the 1934 World Series against the Detroit Tigers. His brother Paul also had won 19 games and two more in the Series. Diz was asking for more than Cardinals' General Manager Branch Rickey was offering. By then living in Bradenton, Florida, the Deans were interviewed by New York World-Telegram sportswriter Joe Williams.

"It is now necessary to refer to the Deans as plural these days," he wrote. "Mr. Dizzy does the pitching and golfing; Mrs. Dizzy does the managing and looking after. She talks like one of these 'he-can't-hurt-us' boxing managers. Everything is '*We* said to Mr. Branch Rickey ... or Mr. Rickey said to *us*.'

"No prize-fighter ever had a manager who looked after him more earnestly or energetically, either," Williams continued.

At first, Rickey would not talk contract with Dizzy if Mrs. Dean was present. Patricia very quickly took care of that little matter. "All I'm trying to do is see that my husband gets what's coming to him," she told Williams. "If that's a crime, they ought to take me out and shoot me because I'm going to keep doing it."

A couple of years after Dizzy passed away, Pee Wee Reese and I were at the winter baseball meetings in New Orleans, Louisiana. We decided to drive over to Wiggins, Mississippi, and see Patricia. We had lunch and spent a couple of hours talking, with Pat doing most of it.

"One thing that has really annoyed me all these years," she admitted, "was to hear people say that without me, Dizzy Dean would never have amounted to anything, that I made him toe the line, that I made every financial decision of his career, and that if anyone wanted to do something, they had to talk to his wife first. Some of that was true."

There was something else she wanted to make perfectly clear.

"Dizzy Dean became a successful pitcher on his own," she continued. "I never struck out a batter or won a ball game for him in his entire career. The ingredients for greatness were in Dizzy from the very beginning. The decisions that were made for our well being were always discussed between us."

Then she looked directly at Pee Wee and me.

"You two worked with Dizzy for years," she said. "You know how stubborn and pigheaded he could be!"

Simultaneously, as if on cue, Pee Wee and I spoke up, "OH NO, PAT. NOT LOVABLE OL' DIZ!"

She ignored that and continued, "When Dizzy made up his mind about something, he was tougher to move than a damn Missouri mule!"

We asked if they ever had any major disagreements.

"Are you kidding?" Patricia replied. "Of course, there were! Who the hell doesn't have arguments with his wife? The only difference was that our battles would sometimes get into the papers. All I will take credit for is steering him in the right direction. That's what any woman would do for the man she married."

Patricia Dean died in Hattiesburg, Mississippi, in 1981 – seven years after Dizzy. I have no doubts that wherever they are, she is still looking after him. Patricia wouldn't have it any other way.

Fresh off the 1934 World Series title, Dizzy Dean and wife Pat enjoy a moment the next winter in their Bradenton, Florida home.

Making music together, Dizzy strums the ukulele for Pat at their home in Florida.

Dizzy and Pat Dean quickly made local friends and often invited them to their Bradenton home for cards.

Still celebrating the Cardinals' 1934 World Series title, Pat Dean took this photo of hero-husband Dizzy just before Christmas.

Having been traded from the Cardinals to the Chicago Cubs as damaged goods, the arm-weary Dizzy was shipped from the Windy City to Tulsa, Oklahoma, in 1940 for rehab. The smiles belie this moment in Dizzy Dean, the baseball player. From then on, most of Dizzy's shining moments came off the diamond.

Dean family collection, courtesy of Gene Kirby

Pat Dean loved her man, which meant she was interested in fishing. These 1940s dock-side shots from Lake Texoma, north of Dallas, show Pat understood white bass and crappie angling, as well as the benefits of a sharp fillet knife.

In this 1961 photo from Phoenix, Pat Dean admires the game scorecards from Dizzy's remarkable 30 pitching wins for the Cardinals in 1934.

Ever the performer, Dizzy Dean lounges with wife Pat on a 1950s vacation in Hawaii.

In 1956, with Dizzy Dean's broadcast career rising to new heights, he cuts the cake with Pat, while celebrating their 25th anniversary in New York City.

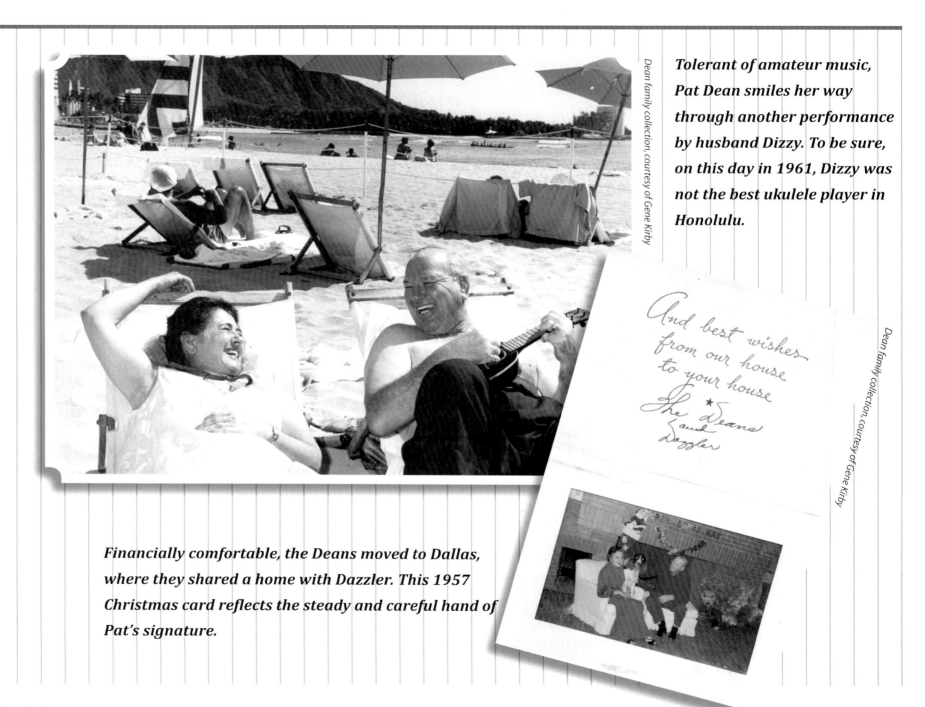

Tolerant of amateur music, Pat Dean smiles her way through another performance by husband Dizzy. To be sure, on this day in 1961, Dizzy was not the best ukulele player in Honolulu.

And best wishes
from our house
to your house
The Deans
*5
Zand
Dazzler

Financially comfortable, the Deans moved to Dallas, where they shared a home with Dazzler. This 1957 Christmas card reflects the steady and careful hand of Pat's signature.

Dean family collection, courtesy of Gene Kirby

Dean family collection, courtesy of Gene Kirby

Dean family collection, courtesy of Gene Kirby

Barbecue is as popular in Pat Dean's home state of Mississippi as anywhere in America. Here, Dizzy and Pat enjoy a lighter moment in the 1960s with friends and a Southern grill master.

Always a bit restless, Dizzy Dean was quick to go hunting, fishing or to dress up during a Caribbean cruise, as he did on this 1960s trip with wife Pat.

Surrounded by baseball honors, Pat and Dizzy Dean pose for a mid-1960s family portrait in their Dallas home.

Part VI

Always Playing the Part

LIVING LARGE TO THE VERY LAST

★

His playing days long gone, Dizzy Dean left the broadcast booth for good in 1966, but the unblinking eye of public attention followed this colorful character, in part because nobody knew what Diz would do or say next. And we loved him for it. As America's favorite son, when the product of an Arkansas sharecropper farm left the broadcast booth, he still had some living to do, and live he did. His own way.

Beyond the microphone but never beyond his own skin, Dizzy, in no particular order, would buy a ranch near Kaufman, Texas, play a mean game of golf, hobnob with Mickey Mantle and other celebs, fish and hunt, sit for interviews and move with wife, Pat, to her hometown of Bond, Mississippi.

Once back in semi-rural Dixie, Dizzy would see his life come full circle. Returned to his roots, he could put his arm around a stranger and call him or her "Podnah."

Now comfy as an old fielder's glove, Diz became just as busy as ever lending

Stage fright? Not these guys. In a 1950s nightclub performance, the spotlight was shared by a star-studded cast; (left to right) Yankees outfielder Mickey Mantle, golfer Dr. Cary Middlecoff, Dizzy Dean, comedian Bob Hope, football star Doak Walker and entertainer Sammy Kaye.

his name to a "filling station" and a charcoal company. He also made mortal enemies in small-town Mississippi, as the recognizable name whispered in a gambling scandal. Once exonerated, Dizzy heard his name bandied about as a candidate for governor, a political position he never sought.

Along the way, Dizzy never passed up a camera, nor a chance to make somebody laugh. To the day he was buried in southern Mississippi, we see that Jay Hanna "Dizzy" Dean simply could not – or would not – be ignored. – *Mark S. McDonald*

DIZZY GETS HIS BADGE

In 1947 while visiting Gene Moore, a former Dodgers and Braves outfielder in Laurel, Mississippi, Dizzy was welcomed by the town officials, who thanked him for all the nice things he had

been saying on television about the great state of Mississippi.

He was also given a badge making him an honorary member of the Laurel police force. "I'm proud of this badge, Mr. Mayor," Dean told the city Mayor and a large gathering, "but I jest want y'all to know that I ain't gonna arrest nobody … Folks has been too nice to me and my wife, Pat."

A FRIENDLY GOLF MATCH

Playing golf one day with a friend who was a big bettor and very proud of his game, Dizzy was losing by a stroke. The sum of $2,000 was riding on this game. His opponent had a three-foot putt to win it all.

As they approached the 18th green, Dizzy walked toward the ball farthest away from the pin and bent over it. His opponent walked over to the ball nearest

the hole and tapped it into the cup – for all intents and purposes winning the match and the $2,000. Dean called a halt.

Dizzy Dean may be mugging for the camera in this 1958 photo, and often played social rounds with movie stars, singers and professional athletes. But the sly right-hander, always a fierce competitor, was not above tricks of gamesmanship.

"Podnah," he said, "I'm sorry, but I'm gonna have to pull the rule book on ya right here. You jest done hit the wrong ball. That wuz my ball you hit into the cup!"

He was right, too. What Ol' Diz had done was deliberately stand over the wrong ball. Penalty stroke. Match over.

DEAN'S 1966 VISIT TO LUCAS

Dizzy waxed philosophical as we visited Lucas, Arkansas, in 1966. "First time I've been back here in many years," Ol' Diz said as we drove around to the place where his house once stood. "Lucas ain't even on the map no more."

We had driven down from St. Louis because Dean wanted to take what he said would probably be the last look at the town where he was born.

Ralph Dennis was Dizzy's teacher. Diz remembered his name because he didn't have many teachers. He dropped out after the third grade. "Mr. Dennis was cross-eyed and chewed tobacco all his life," Dean said. As we neared Dennis' house, Dizzy spotted his old instructor outside filling a bucket of water.

"Gene, that's him," Dean said, "and he ain't changed a bit. He's got a straw hat on, and he's got them overalls on that's got patches all over it."

"I couldn't teach that boy nothing," Dennis said. "I got him through the third grade, but all he was interested in was playing baseball. I had his nose up against the blackboard more than any other boy in school. When the bell rang, all the other students would go out the door into the hall, but Dizzy would jump out the window and head straight to the ball field."

Later, Dizzy told me one day he played hooky.

"Before I coulda git outta the school yard, Ralph Dennis caught me," he said, "because I couldn't get under the barbed wire fence, and he give me a whippin'! When I git home, Dad had heard about it and give me another whippin'."

HALL OF FAME ADDITION

Dean family collection, courtesy of Gene Kirby

In 1953, when he was inducted into baseball's Hall of Fame, Dizzy Dean was depicted as a hayseed from Boondocks, USA - which he was. But he took the event seriously, dressed the part and was genuinely grateful for the recognition.

When Dizzy Dean was voted into baseball's Hall of Fame in 1953, a cartoon was published in the newspapers showing him as a poor little country boy. He was wearing a straw hat, barefoot, chewing on a piece of straw.

"I'm doggone happy to be up here with all them thar mortals in the Hall of Fame!" read the caption.

A country music fan, Dizzy Dean struck up lasting friendships with the likes of Gene "The Singing Cowboy" Autry. In this 1960s vintage photo, Dizzy belts out the "Wabash Cannonball" with his buddy, Roy Acuff, perhaps his all-time favorite.

Dean family collection, courtesy of Gene Kirby

DIZZY AND ROY ACUFF

It was Dizzy Dean who put the tag "King of the Hillbillies" on Roy Acuff. It was later refined to "King of Country and Western Music." Back in the 1940s, Dizzy was in Dallas with Gene Autry attending a Country and Western music show starring Acuff.

Roy introduced both Dean and Autry and had them come on stage to say a few words. Ol' Diz didn't say much (for a change) except to mention how happy he was to be on the same stage with Roy Acuff and Gene Autry.

It was the start of a long friendship and a mutual admiration relationship with Acuff that lasted until Dizzy passed away in 1974. Roy came down from Nashville and was a pallbearer at Dean's funeral in Wiggins, Mississippi. He was asked to sing one of Dizzy's favorite songs, "Precious Memories." Acuff declined.

"I just didn't think I could get through

Always in public demand, even long after his playing days, Dizzy Dean played to the crowd in every event, including a 1948 charity outing in Washington, D.C. Sharing this light moment were Babe Didricksen Zaharias (left), regarded by many as the best all-around female athlete of her time, and Helen Dettweiler.

it without breaking down," Acuff said, "and I didn't want to do that."

ON THE GOLF COURSE

Roy Acuff at one time was involved in the ownership of a golf course at Dunbar Cave near Clarksville, Tennessee. Dizzy came to visit many times to play in charity tournaments. The crowds always followed Ol' Diz and Roy around the course.

At one point in a match, Dean asked him, "Podnah, this looks like a dogleg to the left, but whereabouts is the hole?"

"Dizzy, to be truthful," Roy answered, "I really don't know!"

"Folks, I guarantee y'all one thing," Ol' Diz shouted to the crowd, "Roy Acuff is the only feller I know who owns a doggone golf course and don't even know where the holes is!"

DEAN GETS BEAN-ED

Many years ago, Dizzy was a guest on the radio news show featuring the erudite commentator, H.V. Kaltenborn.

During the interview Dean kept referring to H.V. as "Mr. COTTONBAUM, Mr. CATTLEBAUM, Mr. CATTLONMGBAUM, and Mr. KATTZENBAUM." All this name

In the presence of a camera or microphone, Dizzy Dean might do or say most anything. In this 1952 interview, Milwaukee Braves lefty Warren Spahn just might have been the latest victim of a Dizzy spoof.

calling really irritated H.V. He finally got even by calling Ol' Diz "Mr. Bean!"

Dizzy told me later that Mr. KATTLINGBAUM (Kaltenborn) asked him a question, "Mr. Bean, what do you think about the relationship the United States has at the present time with Russia?" H.V. just knew the answer would be nothing.

Without a moment's pause, Dizzy replied, "Mr. KURLINGBAUM, I'd have Joe Stallion (Stalin) learn them Russian kids the game of baseball. When Mr. Stallion found out how much money he could make in baseball, he'd stop them kids from playing with guns and rifles and get them into an 'honest to God business!' "

Kaltenborn closed with "thank you, Mr. Bean."

Interview over.

HALL OF FAME FIRESTORM

Dean family collection, courtesy of Gene Kirby

*The Halls of Fame are wide open
And they are always full.
Some go in by the door called "push,"
And some by the door called "pull!"
Stanley Baldwin (1867-1947)*

Producer Gene Kirby, who wrote much of this manuscript and compiled archive photos, works a 1941 Mutual Broadcast Game of the Week with Al Helfer and Dizzy Dean. When voted to the Hall of Fame in 1953, Dean was nudged by wife Pat to join Helfer in calling the Hall of Fame game in his honor.

The election of Dizzy Dean to the Hall of Fame in Cooperstown, New York, in 1953 touched off a storm of controversy.

It was in keeping with the rest of his baseball and broadcasting career. The furor resulted from what many sports notables believed was Dizzy's right to be included in such select company. Other greats not voted in that year were, among others, Joe DiMaggio, Bill Terry, Dazzy Vance, Ted Lyons, Gabby Hartnett, Hank Greenberg and Joe Cronin. All have since been inducted.

Some writers who did not vote for Dean felt that his career as a broadcaster was solely responsible for his popularity in gaining admission to the Hall. They quoted Dean's lifetime statistics: he pitched 12 years, of which 5 were complete seasons; appeared in 317 games; won 150 and lost 83; though he led the National League in strikeouts in four of his first five years, Ol' Diz never struck out more than 199 batters in one season.

Consider these for Dean's other credentials: first NL pitcher to strike out 17 batters in a nine-inning game in 1933; only pitcher to get two hits in one inning in World Series history in 1934; and averaged 24 wins in his first five years in the league. With the St. Louis Cardinals, he was voted the Most Valuable Player in the National League in 1934 and received the Most Courageous Athlete of the Year Award in 1938 as a member of the Chicago Cubs.

What did Dizzy Dean have to say about all the stories that he "did not belong" in the Hall of Fame? His answer was simple and to the point. "I didn't have no vote," he said. "I didn't do no campaignin' for it, and 75 percent of them writers who voted for me must have thought I belonged in there – just like I did!"

As the years go by and sports buffs talk about players in the Hall of Fame, for the most part they will discuss their statistics. When Dizzy's name is mentioned, the debate may be about when Ol' Diz defied the President of the National League and wouldn't apologize to him for something he (Dean) said he didn't do, or when Dizzy told those Braves and Dodgers teams in their clubhouses before a game exactly how he was going to pitch to them and then won those two games!

Then there were those great pitching duels between Dizzy and Carl Hubbell of the New York Giants when they were in their primes and the time when Pepper Martin and Dean made a bonfire down the right field foul line when the temperature in St. Louis was almost 100 degrees, and so on …

That is how Dizzy Dean wanted to be remembered, anyway: no STATICS (statistics) when talking about Ol' Diz!

Lest anyone think that the comments regarding Dean's induction into the Hall of Fame were all negative, it was just not the case. Arthur Daley of the New York Times wrote: "Things should be a lot livelier in the Hall of Fame from now on. The brash, impudent and ever-laughing Dizzy Dean has arrived as a full-fledged member, and the place will never be the same again. There was never anything modest about

Baseball has a way of gracefully spanning gaps in time. The day Dizzy Dean was inducted into the Hall of Fame, he savored the 1953 moment with (left to right) pipe-smoking ex-pitcher Cy Young, immortal manager Connie Mack and slugging outfielder Aloysius "Al" Simmons.

him. For five blazing years, the buoyant Mr. Dean was exactly what he said he was – the best! Unfortunately, the records do not quite present an accurate picture of Diz.

"With his easy pitching motion, his overpowering fastball, his courage, his skill, and his utter disdain for all hitters, he probably would have lasted another decade if he hadn't gotten hurt. The self-confessed Great Man is a welcome addition to the Hall of Fame, though he lowers the humility quotient of the immortals to virtually nothing."

Harold Rosenthal of the New York Herald Tribune noted: "Dizzy Dean's elevation to the Hall of Fame is another step along the road he has traveled since his cotton-picking days in Arkansas and his mule-tending days in the pre-World War II Army. Dean now has oil investments, a 300-acre farm outside of Dallas and a new home in the fashionable Brookhollow section of that city. He can, if he chooses, throw away those white 10-gallon hats he wears instead of having them cleaned. Dizzy is unquestionably the most forceful exhibit that foes of 'book larnin' can offer."

And from a United Press International wire dispatch: "The wording on the plaque honoring Dizzy Dean in Baseball's Hall of Fame might easily read this way:

"He had a heart as big as his head, and, brother, that's a lot of heart!"

Dean's election, while other great stars with superior records are on the outside, may lead to quite a controversy. He got himself into enough hot water while he was playing to float a battleship. When Dizzy was traded by the St. Louis Cardinals to the Chicago Cubs in 1938, some of his new teammates resented the fact that he was a sore-armed pitcher drawing a big salary.

Cub's owner Phil Wrigley said, 'Dizzy Dean is a greater asset to the club with a sore arm than a strong-armed pitcher with no heart at all.' That ended that."

Milton Gross of the New York Post wrote: "Baseball's Hall of Fame is part museum and part mortuary, but they really let a live one in yesterday when Dizzy Dean was enshrined. Diz now makes Cooperstown more than a memory. He makes it a part of Americana, which is the way it should be, because the heritage of our athletics is more than a do-or-die spirit. It's as much frolic as it is muscles, as much a chuckle as a chase. This is the essence of all sport, and nobody reflected

it better than Diz, who became wealthy throwing his fastball past the hitters and later describing the way others tried to do it but never losing his sense of humor while doing it."

Grantland Rice, the popular syndicated sports columnist, also put the election of Dizzy Dean into the Hall of Fame into its proper perspective. "After all, the Hall of Fame is not measured entirely in terms of batting, fielding and pitching averages. Dizzy Dean had a brief career, but in his career he left his imprint on the game far beyond many others who had longer and better records."

Dizzy and his wife, Patricia, arrived in Cooperstown on July 27, 1953, for the induction of Diz and Al Simmons (great outfielder of the Philadelphia Athletics) into the Hall of Fame. The ceremonies back then took place in the morning with the exhibition game between two major league teams played in the afternoon. I was there as the producer for the Mutual Game of the Day radio broadcast that Al Helfer and Dizzy aired coast to coast.

For several days prior to the event, Dean had vigorously opposed working the game, figuring that going into the Hall would be enough for one day. Patricia

It was fitting that wife Pat would accompany Dizzy Dean to his induction to the Baseball Hall of Fame in 1953. For years during Dizzy's playing days, Pat was one of the few wives allowed to travel with the team.

finally convinced him to do it for the sake of the fans. He couldn't disappoint them. In all humility he had to tell the nationwide audience that he really belonged. His acceptance speech didn't disappoint them, either.

Dean was introduced by George Trautman, president of the National Association of Professional Baseball Leagues. When presented with his plaque, Diz thanked his wife and teammates. "I also want to thank the good Lord for givin' me a strong back, a strong right arm and a weak mind!"

It was the first time that Dizzy Dean publicly admitted he had ever needed any outside help!

SCORING A HAT TRICK FOR DIZ

★

In the broadcast booth or out, Dizzy Dean and his sidekick Gene Kirby had their share of fun. Several times during Falstaff Brewing promotional trips they were supplied willing ground support from Falstaff marketing exec Gus Gagel and his wife, Dee.

Even well into her 80s, the widowed Dee Gagel remained spry, mostly independent and quite attractive, with a hint of whimsy that dated back to yesteryear. Decades after the fact, Dee chuckled when she recalled the rollicking times she and her husband had when hosting Dizzy and Kirby in their Nebraska home.

One evening, while socializing in an Omaha tavern – Dizzy rarely, if ever, drank alcohol – the group was having an extra-good time when an interloper

Courtesy of Gus and Dee Gagel family collection

Dizzy Dean enjoys dinner with (left to right) Gene Kirby, Pat Vorda and Gus Gagel in the Gagel's Omaha home. Dee Gagel shot this photo in 1957, and saved it all these years. A public figure, Dizzy could become a target for strangers who might play fast and loose with his fame.

photo by Mark S. McDonald

Octogenarian Dee Gagel, now living in Colorado, remembers an evening long ago in Omaha that could have gone badly for Dizzy Dean.

threatened to bust up the party. That is, a woman approached Dizzy and snatched his beloved Stetson off his head. Uh-oh.

Two things you don't do: you don't ask how many acres a man owns, nor do you mess with his hat. Then as now, for any self-respecting fella west of the Mississippi, a hat is more than protection from the sun – it is the very symbol of his manhood, a public measure of his testosterone level, for all to see. Boys don't wear hats; boys wear caps. A man wears a hat.

So it was with Dizzy, whose fine beaver hats were custom-fit for him by friends at the Stetson factory near Dallas. His lid had become as much a part of his persona as his fastball had once been. This sneak attack, then, left Dizzy in a quandary, and not without reason.

He could ignore the transgression, and go on feeling plumb naked until the hat could be replaced. Or, he could go for the quick remedy, which carried considerable risk.

He could try to retrieve his hat, which the stranger was hoping he would do. Obviously deep in her cup and seeking attention, she would almost certainly raise holy hell. While the revelry continued, Dizzy began to stew in silence, rare for him. What to do, what to do?

Knowing the festering brouhaha that would bring negative publicity, Diz pondered his plight ... Do I risk an ugly incident, to save my hat? Just then, a solution came to Diz in thought bubble.

"Mizzz Gagel," Dizzy said, leaning over to lay out the sugar as only he could do, "could you get my hat back?"

Her blue eyes crackling like the Northern Lights, Dee recalled how she nodded quietly and waited for her moment. Then, once the trouble-maker's attention was diverted to the next round of drinks, Dee swooped in with a flight of finesse, whisked the hat off the offending head and returned it to its rightful owner. Public scene avoided.

"Dizzy had as much charisma in person as he had on TV," Dee said of the star pitcher's camera presence. During Falstaff promotions, Dizzy often gave "humorous talks with a little motivation thrown in."

Entertaining as he could be, however, Dee recognized another side of Dizzy.

"He was not always agreeable. Gus would have to wheedle things out of him." And there was one request, in particular, that could make Dizzy balk – singing "Wabash Cannonball."

"Dizzy would get tired of his celebrity role, because strangers were always coming up to him, interrupting dinner to get his autograph," Dee said from her apartment in Castle Rock, Colorado. "But Gus or Gene would keep working on him to sing, saying 'people are here just to hear you sing that song, Diz. You can't disappoint them.'"

Dizzy would cave, and to raucous applause, he would grab the nearest microphone and belt out the tune that he helped make famous. Dizzy would buzz the tower of a rival batter, he would threaten to quit during contract talking, he'd duck a dinner check and belittle his own teammates in the press. One thing Jay Hanna Dean did not do – ignore the common folks. His adoring fans.

"Dizzy was a kind man, always trying to make people laugh," Dee said. "But he was happiest when he was on the golf course, winning money. Guys would line up to lose money to him.

"When Dizzy was coming to town, he would call ahead and tell Gus to set up the tee times. 'Tell those guys to get their golf clubs and their money ready. I'm coming to town.'"

Local pigeons were delighted to get fleeced by a visiting celebrity, Dee said with a chuckle.

"They seemed thrilled to death to lose their money. They could brag to their friends they had played golf with Dizzy Dean."

Dizzy's wife, Pat, ever the shadow, would sometimes intercede.

"You don't have to write this," Dee said, cocking her head, "but Pat wore the pants in that family. Pat was a nice lady, but when it all got too much, she would shield the public from Dizzy. She ruled the roost, you might say."

Then in a moment of hesitation, Dee raised her palm to a busy notepad and pen. Ever the lady, she said, "Oh … don't write that."

One thing for sure: Dee grew up on the national pastime rooting for her hometown St. Louis Browns. By the time she and her late husband became a regular item, Dee was a true baseball fan, dipped and vaccinated.

"I went out with some of the guys back then … the players, I mean," Dee said, dropping her glance and smiling at a distant memory she did not share.

A local girlfriend of hers used to consort with Don Larsen, in 1953 a 23-year-old Browns rookie who would go on to Yankees fame with a 1956 World Series perfect game no-hitter. One night, Dee and Gus showed their friends a couple of after-hours places in St. Louis. By the time Larsen and his date got back to his place, it was 7 in the morning.

"Don got in big trouble over that one," Dee said with a tee-hee. Even 60-something years removed, she clearly finds entertainment in the pranks of yesteryear.

Popular with young and old, Dizzy Dean entertains the Gagel daughters, Sherry, now Sherry Baker of Eldorado Hills, California, and Bonnie, now Bonnie Tomasek of Sedalia, Colorado. Dizzy was the evening guest of Dee and Gus Gagel, who then worked in promotions in Omaha for Falstaff Brewing.

From St. Louis, Gus and his bride were moved to San Jose where his Falstaff career took off. By osmosis, Dee became a huge Giants fan who followed sluggers Willie Mays and Willie McCovey. Later, the Gagels were transferred again and again, before winding up in Omaha. Through it all, Dizzy Dean was a focus of Falstaff promotions.

"For Gus, Dizzy was his biggest project," she said, adding that Gene Kirby's support in keeping Dizzy on track was always welcome.

"Gene was always nice to me. Very nice," Dee said. "We always had a wonderful time when he and Dizzy came to town."

In the last three-quarter century or so, Dee has seen plenty of changes in American culture and, with it, the explosion of media, entertainment and sports. Like so many who have gone before, she is not altogether pleased. Baseball, especially, she liked better when the World Series was played in sunlight.

"Money is now a big, big factor," she said. "Dizzy never made the kind of money the kids do today.

"There is so much involved (agents, endorsements, accountants, attorneys), baseball has changed. The players even started using dope … Steroids, I mean. I used to be a Barry Bonds fan. When his name got mixed up in all that stuff, it upset me very much.

"The U.S. and baseball are not the same as they were years ago. But I still love the game."

Just then, Dee looked up at the TV, flickering across the room, on mute. Her Rockies have just taken a one-run lead over the Reds. – *Mark S. McDonald*

ARKANSAS PENTHOUSE

Many times when talking about his house in Lucas, Arkansas, where he was born, Dizzy would tell someone he lived in a penthouse. Then he would clarify that statement.

"Y'all know what a Arkansas penthouse is?" he would say. "That's a hog pen with Venetian blinds."

BACK HOME IN LUCAS

In 1968 Dizzy Dean and I drove to Lucas, Arkansas, where Dizzy was born.

He had a personal appearance to do in Memphis, but he wanted to go back to Lucas because he hadn't been there in many years. He also made sure that the car we would be in was a big gold and black Cadillac. He drove most of the way until we got within a few miles of Lucas, and then I took over. I drove into town, and he was sitting in the back seat. You could have likened the trip to the return of King Farouk of Egypt!

Driving down those country roads and seeing broken-down shacks where most of the people lived put Dean in a very somber mood. I turned around to him.

"Podnah, are you all right?" I asked.

"Yah, I'm okay," he said, "but what I'm lookin' at makes me very DESPONDENCY (despondent), and I'm talkin' about all them DAPIL-LATED (dilapidated) houses."

Then I said something about the mailboxes in front of those shacks not having any names on them.

"Podnah," he said, "what the hell do they need names on 'em for? Everybody knows where they LIVES!"

"IT AIN'T BRAGGIN' …"

Ol' Diz often spoke about what he was going to do on the mound and then went out and did it. One prediction he made was the surest and safest one of all.

"There will never be another one like me!"

Never short on bravado, Dizzy Dean claimed he could master just about anything. In 1935, he would have been out of his league, however, in a challenge match with British tennis stars Katherine Stammers (left) and Winifred "Freda" James.

During the 1934 World Series, Dizzy Dean shares a laugh with comedian Joe E. Brown. Dizzy signed the print for Kevin "Rusty" Kirby.

Posing for a camera came early and easily for Dizzy Dean. To his left in this 1934 shot are St. Louis Cardinals star Joe Medwick and George "Spanky" McFarland, age 7, child star in "Our Gang" comedy shorts later made for the TV series "The Little Rascals."

Just as witty Will Rogers claimed he "never met a man he didn't like," Dizzy Dean made friends with every cameraman he saw. Here Dizzy clowns with a toy tiger after his Cards beat Detroit in the 1934 World Series.

Players posed for so many hokey publicity shots, the 1934 World Series must have been something of an afterthought. Hard to imagine these antics in today's baseball, even from the next Dizzy Dean.

When Dizzy Dean (right) was the toast of the town, New York had two National League clubs, the Giants and Dodgers. Dean's 1935 St. Louis teammates Ripper Collins (left) and Pepper Martin salt a melon for world heavyweight boxing champ Jack Dempsey at his popular restaurant in New York City.

Dizzy Dean and Babe Ruth. In this 1935 photo at Braves Field (left) and the '36 shot at Lakewood Country Club in St. Petersburg, Florida, these two baseball stars were drawn together. On the field they were dynamic. Off the field they shared a common bond, both coming from poor, broken homes.

In 1946, Dizzy Dean shared a North Hollywood tee box with Bob Hope. In '50, Dizzy played a Dallas course with links legend Ben Hogan and noted touring pro Jimmy Demaret. It is presumed the latter game was a bit more serious.

In 1948, Joe Louis was heavyweight boxing champion of the world. Here, in the notes taken by Gene Kirby, the champ flexes for the benefit of Dizzy Dean and France Laux.

Joe. Louis. Dizzy Dean - France Laux
1948   St. Louis

Louis was raised in Detroit. Dean always
kidded Joe, about to be made pussycats
out of the Tigers in the 1934 World Series.
Louis & Dean were in their prime in
1933 - 1936.

Gone from the diamond, but not from the public eye, Dizzy Dean displays a ball depicting his highest number of strikeouts in a major league game. He is joined in this 1950s dugout shot by Cleveland right-hander Bob Feller and lefty Herb Score.

In the 1950s, Dizzy Dean was a guest on NBC's Roy and Dale Rogers Show. Among young fans, Roy's horse, Trigger, was well-known, too.

His broadcast fame growing, Dizzy Dean joins wife Pat and Gene Kirby (front passenger seat) for a 1955 Meridian, Mississippi, tribute to singer Jimmie Rodgers.

Johnny Lujack, the 1947 Heisman Trophy-winning Notre Dame quarterback, joins Dizzy Dean at a mid-1950s golf outing in Memphis. Lujack, age 91 at press time, is the oldest living Heisman winner.

Cherry Hills Golf Club in Denver hosted an event that drew President Dwight Eisenhower, Dizzy Dean and other well-known figures such as William Frawley (inset), who starred with Lucille Ball and Desi Arnaz in "I Love Lucy."

When he wasn't clowning with politicians and celebrities, Dizzy Dean was making new friends in baseball. Dizzy in 1953 admired the grit of Yankees manager Casey Stengel (below) and the talent of catcher Bill Dickey.

Jackie Robinson's arrival in 1947 broke the baseball color barrier. By the time he and Dizzy met for this photo in 1955, the Dodgers infielder had changed the game forever.

Hall of Famer Walter Alston managed the Dodgers, reportedly on a series of one-year contracts that lasted more than 20 seasons. One writer credited Alston's longevity to the manager's small ego, saying. "Do you realize how important that is?" Dizzy couldn't have said it better.

With Pee Wee Reese on his left and Dizzy Dean on his right, Yankees manager Casey Stengel in this 1960 shot was surrounded by CBS Game of the Week on-air talent.

When the Yankees won the 1961 American League pennant, the victorious clubhouse was full of horseplay. Festivities were joined by (left to right) Yankees radio announcer Phil Rizzuto, Dizzy Dean, Joe DiMaggio and jubilant manager Ralph Houk.

Dean family collection, courtesy of Gene Kirby

Dean family collection, courtesy of Gene Kirby

C&W singer Porter Waggoner gives Dizzy Dean a big hand during a 1964 performance at the Grand Ole Opry in Nashville. Less than two years later, caught in a CBS-NBC battle for broadcasting rights, Dizzy – more popular at the grassroots than ever – was given the boot.

Though gone from the diamond and the broadcast booth, Dizzy Dean was always welcomed in ballparks nationwide. Here, he shares a 1968 teaching moment in Shea Stadium with Braves coach Satchel Paige, a pitching phenom that Dizzy long admired.

Dean family collection, courtesy of Gene Kirby

Part VII

Living Large to the Very Last

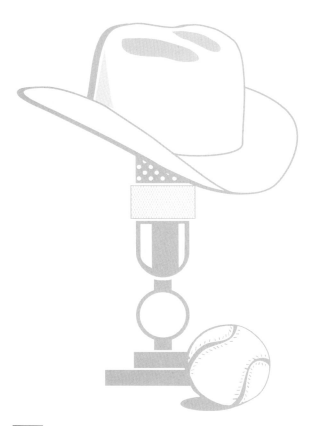

POST PLAYING DAY

By the late 1950s, Dizzy Dean was no longer chasing ghosts from his childhood. He was well-known, fully accepted – often adored – and, yes, rather wealthy. On that score, wife Pat deserves her share of credit.

No longer a regular on TV broadcasts, Dizzy spent his later years like the gentleman farmer-rancher he had become. He owned the land, all right, but true to his nature, Dizzy never did much of the actual work.

Instead, he hunted quail and waterfowl, made public appearances, fished with buddies, visited with old baseball teammates and rivals and traveled with Pat, brother Paul and his wife, Dorothy. And that's only when he wasn't playing golf.

Never one to take it easy, Dizzy mashed the gas pedal of life until the very day he died, suddenly in 1973 at age 64. His fatal attack occurred, as you might guess, during a recreational road trip to Nevada. We figure Dizzy died with his boots on, or maybe his golf spikes. Either way, you can bet he was joking with friends. – *Mark S. McDonald*

Even after his baseball and broadcasting careers wound down, Dizzy Dean was a high-profile visitor anywhere he went. In this shot from the late 1950s, Dizzy creates a pleasant breeze with his neighbors in Wiggins, Mississippi.

BROTHER PAUL AND HIS BELOVED DOROTHY

★

Where one was outgoing, brash, ever thirsty for public attention and the pop of flash bulbs, the other was more modest, low-key, retiring and almost withdrawn. Dizzy Dean and brother Paul were two peas from the same pod, all right, but as similar as a jalapeño and a grapefruit.

Paul cultivated family and a close circle of friends and generally shied from the limelight that Dizzy so vigorously sought. In fact, Paul ducked publicity and was not fond of his nickname "Daffy," invented by writers trying to drum up interest from Americans mired in the Great Depression. Paul rarely cut up in public for the sports writers and photographers that invariably trailed the older sibling. On the diamond, Paul was another story.

Long and lean like his brother, when Paul Dean was healthy, he was nearly as

productive as his Hall of Fame brother, Dizzy. Indeed, their injury-shortened careers with the St. Louis Cardinals ran eerily parallel.

The younger Dean was an All-Star in his own right, compiling a 38-23 record that included a 19-11 mark in the pennant-winning season of 1934, backed with another strong 19-11 the following year.

Deep into middle age, ever-loyal Dizzy Dean played golf and traveled with his younger brother Paul. In this mid-1930s photo, a young Paul Dean and his wife Dorothy enjoy a boat ride in Biloxi, Mississippi.

This flashy start to Paul's Major League career featured two of the Cards' four wins against Detroit in the '34 World Series. It was – and is – the only time in MLB annals that two brothers won four games required for a Series championship.

From the start, Dizzy was his kid brother's biggest fan, the unpaid manager of the Paul Dean marketing/hot air division.

Even as Dizzy was pitching his way to the majors late in his official rookie year in 1931, he began hounding pro scouts in Arkansas and Texas to give Paul a tryout. The humble Paul was eventually given a shot and made good, but not before he had earned his high school diploma in 1931. On his way to the big club in St. Louis, Paul groomed his game with three minor league teams. By the time Paul got the call-up to The Show, he was a finished product. To the surprise of no one, the second Dean was a welcome addition to the Cardinals pitching staff – and an instant success.

In his rookie season, Paul shackled the Brooklyn Dodgers with a no-hitter. Having just won his 28th game of the season in the first of a double-header, Dizzy met with writers in the Cardinal clubhouse after a long and triumphant day. He quickly sent them to scribbling in their notepads.

"Heck," Dizzy deadpanned for quote-hungry writers, "if I'd-a known Paul was going to pitch that no-hitter in the second game, I'd-a thowed a no-hitter in the first game."

So it went for Paul and Dizzy, leading the Cardinals with a display of sizzling fastballs and benders that sent rival batsmen into muttering U-turns back to the dugout … but not for long.

Just as Dizzy's career was clipped by injuries, Paul suffered the same fate. Two seasons of glory for Paul morphed into a long list of arm ailments and assorted other injuries.

For seven seasons, from 1935-39 with the Cardinals, then 1940 and '41 with the New York Giants, Paul became unreliable in a regular starting rotation. Shipped down to the minor league Houston Buffaloes in '42, Paul raised eyebrows by making 30 starts and eating up 219 innings en route to a fashionable 19-8 record. Alas, he was doing it, not with the heater that made both Deans famous, but with guile and a variety of lukewarm off-speed deliveries.

In 1943 the American League St. Louis Browns took one last sample of the damaged goods. It did not go well, for Paul or the Browns.

Even with U.S. locked in the deadly World War II and the national pasttime diluted by top players having enlisted with Uncle Sam, Paul lasted only three appearances. The Browns released him and, at age 30, Paul was out of baseball.

Paul Dean – like brother Dizzy and so many pitchers before and since – had been a young skyrocket that burst on the scene, then flamed out and fell just as quickly into baseball darkness. But save your sympathy.

Unlike too many other ballplayers, however, Paul played the game of life that was not entirely defined by chalk foul lines.

Never much of a high-stakes gambler – unless he was playing golf with Dizzy and pals – Paul managed his money and invested wisely. Paul for 35 years owned a home in Dallas and variously returned to a weekend apartment in Springdale, Arkansas. There he also owned an auto service center, along with a farm at nearby Lake Village, Arkansas. In between, Paul made public appearances, built houses in Dallas and owned minor league franchises. Just as importantly, Paul was lucky in love.

In 1935, while the younger Dean was loafing during the off-season, he met and soon married the former Dorothy Miller Sandusky of Eudora, Arkansas, a college student. Theirs was a whirlwind, two-month courtship, ending with the smitten Paul dashing off to nearby Fort Smith to buy a wedding ring.

Published reports from the day say the couple had planned to be married in a late-afternoon ceremony in Russellville, but Paul's rushed-up trip to Fort Smith took longer than he expected. Not until 8 p.m., so the story goes, did the breathless groom arrive with the ring so the happy couple could exchange vows in extra innings.

During it all, a reporter somehow got wind that a World Series hero was about to marry a local girl. Paul, enormously busy at the moment and understandably preoccupied, was asked what Dizzy would think of his kid brother's sudden announcement. Paul's reply, per usual, was direct and to the point – a strike, right down the middle:

"It is none of his business anyhow."

For her part, Dorothy, a beauty contest winner still in her teens, had started studying journalism, with hopes of graduating and becoming a reporter. Instead, she got married, honeymooned in Gulfport, Mississippi with Dizzy and Pat Dean, and opted for a life in baseball.

For Dorothy, bright and beautiful, throwing in with a ballplayer represented something of a risk. Ballplayers of yester-year, especially minor leaguers, didn't make the serious hedge fund-type money they do today. Months of travel and schedule-induced separations could take their toll on a marriage, especially newlyweds.

Dorothy never regretted, at least publicly, not finishing her college degree.

"All of the travel was by train," Dorothy told an Associated Press reporter in Tulsa during a 1972 interview. "I would pack a trunk, stay in a hotel three or four days, then repack the trunk and put it back on the train and go on."

Dorothy traveled with the team until the first of their four children was born. After that she limited her baseball travel to home games.

"I love baseball," she said, "always have. When you are married to a Major League baseball star, there is no greater life. Diz and Paul were stars."

Long after his playing days, Paul Dean coached college ballplayers, serving as head coach at the now defunct University of Plano (Texas) from 1965-69.

From her teens to her senior years, Dorothy stood by her man, never blinking at Paul's series of minor league trials and his eventual flameout.

"I wouldn't trade a baseball life for anything, not even being the wife of the President," she said. "Baseball is all

I know. I have been in it since I was 18. That is why I loved it."

On March 17, 1981, a heart attack claimed Dizzy's brother, the third son of Albert Monroe Dean and Alma Nelson Dean. Paul Dean was 68.

The widowed Dorothy outlived her husband by more than a decade, dying on May 8, 1995. She was 82. She, too, is buried at Oakland Memorial Cemetery in Clarksville, Arkansas.

Today, in repose as in life, the girl with the dashing smile known as "Dot" remains forever linked to husband Paul Dee "Daffy" Dean, and to baseball history.
– *Mark S. McDonald*

A LEAGUE OF HIS OWN – DIZZY DEAN BASEBALL

★

For the record, Dizzy Dean excelled at golf, cards, gambling, and personal appearances. He would tell you so "hisself." National promotions for lead sponsor Falstaff Beer and other products such as Ole Diz Charcoal manufactured by business pals in Wiggins, Mississippi kept the old right hander busy and very much in public view.

Between promo gigs, Dizzy was an avid hunter and fisherman, and he loved to visit New Orleans to eat and party. Other favorite stops were Las Vegas and Reno for high-stakes gambling at most any game of chance.

On the serious side – a side Dizzy rarely revealed – Dean was not much for politics or social movements.

Indeed, once Little League Baseball, based in Williamsport, Pennsylvania, forbade its affiliated leagues from banning black kids, an alternative youth baseball

Once an organization for whites only, Dizzy Dean Baseball, Inc. for decades has welcomed all kids, regardless of race or color. The organization conducts youth baseball championships for boys 6-19 and softball competition for girls 6-18. At its national tournaments, Dizzy Dean Baseball honors a team for sportsmanship, a rarity in youth sports today.

program bearing his name – Dizzy Dean Youth Baseball – sprang up in 1977 in the Deep South. Based in Mississippi and chartered long after its namesake's death, Dizzy Dean Baseball was all-white.

The color line long since broken, the league now called Dizzy Dean Baseball, Inc. now joins Dixie Youth Baseball and Little League in welcoming young players of all ethnicities. According to the organization's website, Dizzy Dean conducts championships for boys aged 6-19 and softball competition for girls 6-18. – *Bo Carter*

DEFINING DIZZY DEAN

Editor's note: Seeds for this book on Dizzy Dean took root in Gene Kirby's fertile mind more than 50 years ago. While the idea was growing, Kirby's son Glenn agreed to collaborate and finish what his aging father had started so long ago. The plan never bore fruit, until now.

While working on the project, Glenn Kirby, having already traveled thousands of miles and contacting the likes of Hall of Famers Paul Waner, Mickey Cochrane and Rogers Hornsby, died in a 1982 car wreck in Grand Junction, Colorado. Earlier that evening, he had just finished interviewing Pee Wee Reese.

Only recently, buried and almost lost under the sheer weight of time and period photographs, we found a packet containing

Author Gene Kirby in 1961 coaxed New York slugger Roger Maris to pose in the tunnel between the Yankees dugout and clubhouse. At left, the late Glenn Kirby and his older brother Kevin Kirby appear to be star-struck, though the kids had no way to know that within the next two hours, Maris would hit his 61st homer, breaking Babe Ruth's record. The print is signed by Maris to Kevin with "best of luck." Good luck, indeed.

Glenn's scribbled notes. Index cards, bar napkins, notebook paper, yellow legal pad, a treasure chest. Much is illegible but – Eureka! – Glenn knew his way around a typewriter, thus salvaging a 1980 summary of his observations of Dizzy Dean and the nation that made him famous.

The editors think the following words from Glenn Kirby are not only spot-on, but they add insight, depth and breadth to a bittersweet project. Perhaps you will agree. – *Mark McDonald*

By Glenn Kirby

I have it! Listening to one of the Dizzy Dean tapes for the millionth time, it finally sunk in. While taking notes and trying to organize his early life, it hits me like a lead balloon.

I remember one statement Dean made regarding his early life, and how he was never invited to parties because he didn't have the things – shoes and nice clothing – the other kids had. How he literally used to stand on the outside,

To many, Dizzy Dean was almost bigger than life, but as this visit to a Dallas hospital indicates, he always seemed to have time for youngsters.

eavesdropping on the parties, and wish he could be on the inside.

Dizzy used to see automobiles going up the road being driven by people who had even less education than he had. And he made a vow that one day he was "gonna have a car and nice clothes, and everybody's gonna want me at parties at their houses."

This was the essential Dizzy Dean – a man molded by the prejudices forged by the social strata of American society, forced to acknowledge that money brings social acceptance ... and declare within himself that education was not necessarily a condition to achieve any of that.

The vehicle for his ascent in society was baseball. The social acceptance was achieved through the money and nationwide exposure in sports broadcasting. His ability

to speak to the masses in his native tongue (and theirs) was the key.

The political calling for governorship in Mississippi in the 1960s, if Dean had been so inclined, may well have blossomed into a campaign to the White House. The changing South, at least in Mississippi, may have proved too much of an obstacle to overcome, but so much for speculation. It boils down to this for the basic intent:

To present a comprehensive overview of Depression Era American society and its psychological effects on an impoverished Arkansas youth ... tracing his climb through baseball's Golden Age and the infancy of sports on TV.

It will be a case study of Dizzy Dean, taking into account the following:

- Cross-cultural influences such as the personality of a child in the class structure of his youth vs. the corporate structure of organized baseball and broadcasting networks.
- The changing social climate in America, the Roosevelt years/social programs/the socialization of America.
- Dean's observations of people/power/money resulting in his personal motivation.
- Role of the media, which catapulted a Dizzy Dean character into baseball

prominence, then later to sports broadcasting.

- To trace the history and direction of baseball from the early days to today's national (big business) pastime. Why baseball is indeed the sport in America, noting the personal nature of the game and (fan identification with) the players, how it transcends social and class boundaries.

Dizzy Dean. Who was this man who so endeared himself in the hearts of so many Americans? He was supremely bold, brash, conceited, self-centered, egotistical – and he would tell you so himself.

Perhaps the key to Dean's success, his appeal to the masses, was his accessibility. He was a classic example of the American success story. The dream lives, and Dean provided it. He started with nothing in the cotton fields of Arkansas and Texas, and dreamed of more. What he accomplished was more than the realization of his own desires, he reaffirmed some basic values

and principles that might have been shaded by recent events.

Dean was not a saint. It would be ludicrous for anyone to think of him in such terms. Perhaps what set this man apart from many was his basic humanity. It certainly was not his humility. He was gifted with a remarkable throwing arm, and even when that arm went dead after such a short career, his mouth carried him to new heights of glory.

For a man with barely a third-grade education, he had an amazing grasp of everything human. His manipulation of the power structure of major networks was unprecedented for the time.

I guess many of us viewed Dizzy as sort of a magician. Once he succeeded in gaining our attention, we sat spellbound, awaiting his next feat. The kind of magic Ol' Diz performed appealed not to just one generation, one class, or one type of people. Rather, it was the magic of forgetting all those differences, and uniting us on a common front of laughter, gamesmanship and revelry.

For a few hours, we could suspend the distractions of reality, and concentration on the much more desirable benefits derived from a ballgame.

The strength and power exuded by Dean could not help but transfer to his audience. He provided us with hope for the Depression days when the Gashouse Gang fought everyone, including themselves, all for the No. 1 spot in baseball. He reminded us to remember where we came from and where we were going, the values of family, truth and honesty. He never forgot his childhood home in Lucas, Arkansas, nor did he forget the people who down through the years never yielded in their solid support for him as "one of their own."

Dean gave us a weekly family picnic in front of that TV set – father and son, wife, mother, sister and relatives – all together, yet each one enjoying something personal.

He gave us the American Dream, and he gave us himself. Dean gave us his strengths and gave us his weaknesses. It was then up to us to pick and choose, to implement which ones had meaning in our own lives.

Dean had his detractors but I challenge any of them, past or present, to deny at least some good in this man.

By 1937, as this photo from a Florida gas station indicates, Dizzy Dean could not go anywhere without drawing attention. Some critics, pointing out that Dizzy pitched only five complete seasons, said his Hall of Fame induction was based more on popularity than achievement.

An Ambassador for baseball, Dizzy Dean (front row, third from left) joins other noted players in 1953 to conduct a youth clinic in Baton Rouge, Louisiana. Well-known big leaguers abound. To the right of Dizzy is Hall of Famer Mel Ott, with pitchers Mel Parnell (second from right) and Bill Lee (far right). Second row: Joe Adcock (second from left), Boo Ferris and Schoolboy Rowe. Back Row second from left are Milt Bolling, next to Grady Hatton and Ted Kluszewski.

Once a boy of the soil, Dizzy Dean by the 1950s had evolved from ballplayer to broadcaster to gentleman farmer and rancher. Dizzy's DD Ranch near Kaufman, Texas, just southeast of Dallas, was a return to his rural roots.

Dizzy Dean and his producer-sidekick Gene Kirby bet the ponies during a Falstaff promotional trip to Omaha in the early 1960s.

In the late 1950s, the Ak-Sar-Ben Racetrack in Omaha held a race to honor a certain baseball star-turned-broadcaster. Winner of the Dizzy Dean Handicap poses for his trophy.

Dean family collection, courtesy of Gene Kirby

His grade school teachers and his military superiors can well attest that Dizzy Dean needed fresh air and plenty of space. Nobody loved hunting more than Dizzy Dean. Quail hunts took him to Arkansas, a pronghorn antelope hunt to New Mexico. Those outings were topped only by the camaraderie of waterfowling with Beaumont, Texas Falstaff distributor Frank Mackin and his son Frank, Jr.

Route 1
Ramhurst Ga
June 27 1953

Mr. Jean Kirby
Mutual Game of the day
Macon, Ga.

Dear Jean ;

1 enjoy the game of the day over W.B.L.J. in Dalton,Ga.
Dizzy and Al really tease you about farming. Why don't you get a yoke and
hitch these two hefty bulls to a bull tongue with heavy Johnson wings and
slow them down.

Welcome to Georgia to all three and come again and often.Cecil Travis
former Washington Senator player is active in Atlanta with the boys baseball
programs. The Atlanta Crackers give free passes to Blood doors in the
Atlanta area.

Best of luck to all you fellows.

Sincerely,

Ben Bright

Ben Bright
Route 1
Ramhurst, Ga.

715 North Jackson
San Angelo, Texas
July 2, 1953

Mr. Gene Kirby
Mutual Game of the Day Program

Dear Mr. Kirby:

I want to give you an assist in stumping Dizzy Dean on
his farming knowledge.

Tell Dizzy that he is plowing a mule to a walking plow and
the plow is running to deep. Then ask him what he must
do to the mule's harness to make the plow run shallow.

He may know the answer. If he does not, then tell him
to move the back-band to the rear on the mule's back
about two links of a trace chain or six inches. That will
help lift the point of the plow up and make it run shallow.

Trusting that this will enable you to rub it in on Dizzy,
I am ,

Sincerely,

E.E. Young

Viewers of CBS Game of the Week in the 1950s and '60s made no secret of their opinions on Dizzy Dean's commentary, his play-by-play man Pee Wee Reese and their producer, Gene Kirby.

Humorist Will Rogers had his own brand of homespun wisdom, a trait widely enjoyed by Dizzy Dean – indeed, all Americans – during the Depression of the mid-1930s. This aging print is signed by Dizzy to the author's son, Glenn Kirby.

Entertainer Joe E. Brown, he of the seemingly rubber face, in 1935 received from Dizzy Dean the Cardinals jersey, game socks and cap he wore in the World Series. Brown eventually gave the memorabilia to the Hall of Fame.

PEE WEE'S FINAL SALUTE

There isn't anyone around today who spent more time with Dizzy Dean than my good friend, Gene Kirby. Rumor has it that Gene has been around so long, he even saw Dizzy pitch in his prime back in the 1930s.

I still remember the day Gene met me coming off the field in Comiskey Park in Chicago after the first game of the 1959 World Series. He asked me how I would like to work with Dizzy Dean on the TV Game of the Week next year. "No, I don't think so," was my first response, but I then said, "Why don't you meet me back at the hotel in an hour or so, and we'll talk about it."

Later, sitting in the hotel lounge, I told Gene that I had never done anything like this. Besides, I had heard that Dizzy was kind of tough to get along with, let alone work with him. He assured me that this wasn't so; that I would get along with Dizzy just fine. He also told me I'd only be working two days

CBS play-by-play man Pee Wee Reese, producer Gene Kirby and color analyst Dizzy Dean fueled the popularity of baseball on TV. As Kirby's vignettes and photos show, and Reese so poignantly wrote, the trio built a bond that lasted for years.

a week on the broadcasts on weekends: leave home Friday morning and be back in Louisville every Sunday night.

Gene also told me that no broadcast experience would not be a big problem, and that he would come to Louisville over the winter and help me any way he could. He also said we would listen to a lot of

tapes and watch some baseball television games. We left it that way, and I told him to call me at home after the Series.

A week later, Dizzy and his wife, Pat, called me. "Podnah," Dizzy said, "it ain't no big deal. I'll hep you all I can." Pat then got on the phone and told me how much she would like to have me come and work with them. I didn't know I would be working with Pat, too!

Still undecided, I called Buzzie Bavasi, the GM of the Los Angeles Dodgers. Buzzie suggested I take the job. "You'll probably screw it up," he said, "but at least give it a try. If it doesn't work out, you can always come back to the Dodgers!"

That was it. I took the job.

In 1935, when he was an off-season salesman in St. Louis, Dizzy Dean flashes the Hall of Fame smile that won over the former Patricia Nash and millions of baseball fans. Author Gene Kirby notes that, posthumously, somebody finally corrected Dizzy's birthdate.

I had known Dizzy a long time. He was with the Chicago Cubs when I first came up with Brooklyn in 1940, but I never got to hit against him. Years later, I told him I wished I had hit against him with that "crap" he threw up there in his later years.

"Pee Wee, I woosht you'da had that privilege," Dizzy said. "I made a pretty good livin' pitchin' against fellers like you."

That winter (1960) the Falstaff Brewing Corp. called a news conference in St. Louis to announce the new broadcasting team for the TV Game of the Week on CBS. Dizzy, at one

Dean family collection, courtesy of Gene Kirby

point early in the conference, relieved me of any tenseness I may have been experiencing when someone asked me a question that I answered by just shaking my head.

Dizzy grabbed the microphone.

"Folks," he began, "my Podnah can't speak, and I don't talk too good myself. I read even worse. So, all I have to say is Ol' Diz and Pee Wee is gonna make one helluva team on TV – that's if anybody kin git around to understandin' what we're talkin' about!"

I can say honestly that the six years I spent with Dizzy and Gene on the Game of the Week were the best years of my professional life. I know you'll enjoy this book about Dizzy Dean as much as I enjoyed being a part of working with those two gentlemen. Gene tells you all about his many years of working with Ol' Diz, and if anyone is qualified to talk or write about him, it's Gene Kirby.

In baseball there is a phrase often used by players to express their feelings about the games they are playing. "We're having fun," they say, almost to a man. Well, Dizzy, Gene and I had it, too: a ton of fun! – *Pee Wee Reese (written in 1977)*

Part VIII

Extra Innings

ACKNOWLEDGMENTS

To my sister, Henrietta Jordan. To my children Kevin, Wendy and Sara and to my former wife Dorothy Hull. All of them kept after me for years to get this book written.

To Bob Broeg, Len Bramson, Pee Wee Reese, Phil Cavarretta, Don Zimmer, Gene Mauch, Bill Sheehan, Joe Durso, Rex Bradley, Randy Lanchner, Al Abrams, Dave Davidow, Arthur Richman, Al Cartwright, Jim Fanning, Seymour Siwoff, Jimmie McDowell, Harry Farrar, Lowell Reidenbaugh, Ray Doan, Bill Gallo, Don Gutteridge, Harold Scherwitz, Jack and Cass Halpin, Larry Shenk, Mary Trank, Bob Bartholomay, Richie Ashburn, Bill Brown, Tom Cheek, Peter Durso, Tom Gorman, Peter Golenbock, Mary Herwitz, Al Lopez, Danny O'Brien, Sid Jacobson, Oliver French, France Laux, Lloyd Gregory, Edna Little, Selma Cotton. Thank you. They all did so much to finally help me make the Dizzy Dean book a reality.

– *Gene Kirby*

THE KIRBY CAREER PATH

Gene Kirby, as he burst on the sports scene in 1941

Gene Kirby had over 50 years of experience in the sports broadcasting field of both radio and television. He was primarily involved in Major League Baseball as broadcaster, director, writer, researcher and producer, but he also worked in college and pro football and basketball.

Major League Baseball "Game of the Week"

- Dizzy Dean, Pee Wee Reese and Buddy Blattner – agency producer, client supervisor, play-by-play announcer and pre-game shows, 12 years
- "Falstaff Baseball Highlights" – writer, producer and technical advisor with Dizzy Dean, Pee Wee Reese and Buddy Blattner, Falstaff Brewing Corp.
- Sports publicity and sports relations consultant – managed personal appearances for Dizzy Dean through Dancer-Fitzgerald-Sample, New York and Falstaff Brewing Corp., 15 years

Career Highlights

- Traveling secretary – Montreal Expos Baseball Club, 1969-70 and 1979
- Executive producer – Philadelphia Phillies Baseball Club (Radio/TV), 1971-73
  WPHL-Ch. 17, produced "Richie Ashburn Pre-Game Show" (TV), 1973
- Vice president of Administration & Director of Broadcasting – Boston Red Sox, 1973-77
- Administrative assistant and director of broadcasting – Montreal Expos, 1978-82
- Radio broadcaster, Toronto Blue Jays, 1983-84
- Consultant on the movie "The Natural," starring Robert Redford, 1983
- Worked and consulted with former baseball players to become broadcasters:

  - Don Drysdale, Los Angeles Dodgers
  - Richie Ashburn, Philadelphia Phillies
  - Bob Montgomery, Boston Red Sox
  - George Kell, Detroit Tigers
  - Jerry Coleman, San Diego Padres
  - Jim Fanning, Montreal Expos
  - "Rusty" Staub, New York Mets
  - Tim McCarver, New York Mets

By 1948, Gene Kirby was well on his way to national assignments. Here he interviews Joe "Ducky" Medwick, former star outfielder with the famed St. Louis Cardinals' Gas House Gang.

1941-1943: Station WCOA, Pensacola, Florida

Chief announcer, assistant manager, program director, news and sports editor. Sports broadcasts:

- Pensacola Fliers baseball
- Golden Gloves Army and Navy boxing matches
- Pensacola Naval Air Station football

1944 - 1950: ABC - Station WJZ, New York

Broadcasts other than sports:

- America's Town Meeting of the Air – Modern Industrial Bank, two years
- Garden of' Song musical show – 4711 Products, Kelly-Nason advertising agency, 1946
- Lone Ranger (local cut-ins) – General Mills, Kenyon & Eckhardt Agency, 1946
- What Do People Think quiz show – National Association of Manufacturers, 1948
- George Sokolsky, News – New York Sun, Victor Bennett Agency, 1948-1949

1950 - 1951: Station WINS, New York – Crosley Broadcasting Corp - Sports Director and writer:

- 15-minute guest sports shows, six days a week
- Two 15-minute sports shows – pre- and post-game for every New York Yankees pro football game, sponsored by the World Telegram and Sun
- Broadcaster, New York pro football games, 1950

Gene Kirby family archives

"Don't get excited, Podners! It's only time for the commercial — but first, a little of the Wabash Cannonball..."

Late prize-winning cartoonist Bill Gallo won national awards for his works in the New York Daily News. In 1960, Gallo depicted the CBS Game of the Week booth with Dizzy Dean in the middle, flanked by producer Gene Kirby at left and play-by-play man Pee Wee Reese.

Radio

1950-1953, Mutual Broadcasting System

"Game of the Day" baseball broadcasts. four years as producer and play-by-play announcer, including pre- and post-game shows

- Play-by-play for Mutual's Game of the Day, 1950
- Contracted to broadcast Mutual Broadcasting System's football "Game of the Week," 1951-1953

1954-60, "Great Moments in Sports," sponsored by the U.S. Air Force, producer, director and writer for more than 100, 15-minute shows, with advertising agencies: Dancer-Fitzgerald-Sample, Ruthrauff & Ryan, McManus, John & Adams. Shows included:

- Roy Riegels' wrong-way run in the 1929 Rose Bowl
- Bobby Thomson's home run in 1951 playoff game
- Joe Louis-Max Schmeling fight, first-round knockout, 1938
- War Admiral-Seabiscuit match race, 1938
- Frankie Crosetti homers off Dizzy Dean, 1938 World Series
- "Cookie" Lavagetto spoils Bill Bevens' no-hit bid, 1947 World Series

"Pee Wee Reese Show" – producer, director and writer of more than 150, five-minute shows, mostly about baseball, sponsored by Falstaff Brewing Corp. with agency Dancer-Fitzgerald-Sample, New York

Gene Kirby worked the broadcast booth for 15 years of Major League Baseball. None of his colleagues was more respected than former Brooklyn Dodgers shortstop Pee Wee Reese (second from right). In 1955, Reese played with some of baseball's immortals (l to r): Duke Snider, Gil Hodges, Jackie Robinson, Roy Campanella.

Other Sports Highlights

- Harry Wismer's Sports Show – Weber & Heilbroner Clothes, 1946

- Spotlight on Sports: 15-minute weekly show on WJZ, New York and the ABC Network – producer and writer with featured interviews and human interest stories of past and present sports personalities, 1947

- New York Giants baseball – WMCA, New York, 1948

- New York Giants pro football games – WJZ-TV, 1948

- Boxing bouts – WJZ-TV, MacArthur Stadium, New York

- Bradley University basketball games and National Invitational Tournament at Madison Square Garden

- Columbia University football games – WINS, New York, announcer, 1948

- Gator Bowl-Columbia University – MBS College Game of Week

- Broadcast New York Giants pro football games with Chris Schenkel – CBS-TV, 1956

- St. Louis: St. Louis Hawks pro basketball play-by-play and color announcer, producer – KMOX-KSD-TV St. Louis, 1956-1960

- U.S. Military Academy (Army) football play-by-play announcer – WINS, West Point, New York, 1967

- Southern Conference college basketball Game of the Week, play-by-play announcer, 1968

- Philadelphia Phillies highlights as writer and producer, 1971-72

Dean family collection, courtesy of Gene Kirby

Personal differences eventually split the broadcast team of Dizzy Dean and Buddy Blattner with Gene Kirby as producer. But Kirby always regarded Blattner as the consummate professional.

Courtesy of Gene Kirby

President Richard Nixon greets Gene Kirby during a 1970 visit to the White House.

Freelance Writer

Published works in the New York Times, Sporting News, Sports Heritage magazine and in the Baseball Scorebook and magazines of the Toronto Blue Jays and New York Yankees.

- Roger Maris: "The Other Number 9"
- Ted Williams: "His Last At Bat"
- Carl Mays/Ray Chapman: "Baseball's Only Fatality"
- Dizzy Dean: "You Ain't Never Left Us, Podnah!"
- Pete Gray: "The One-Armed Wonder"
- Stu Miller: "High on a Windy Hill," 1961 All Star Game
- Gene Mauch: "The Early Years in Montreal"
- Bobby Thomson: "The Shot Heard 'Round the World"

- Robert Redford: "Baseball Goes Hollywood" (The Natural)
- Emil "Dutch" Levsen: "Baseball's Iron Men"

Commercial Announcer
- Sinclair Gasoline - TV and radio
- Vitalis - TV
- Mennen - TV and radio
- Noxema - TV sports spots
- Falstaff Brewing Corp. - TV and radio
- Penn Central RR - Radio
- Wheaties -TV
- ESSO Gasoline - radio

Master of Ceremonies
- Ladies Be Seated (Johnny Olsen) - ABC
- Rumpus Room
- Meet Me in Manhattan
- Society of Amateur Chef's
- John Robert Powers Model Show
- Sammy Kaye's "So You Want To Lead a Band" 1946-1947

As baseball consultant to the classic Hollywood film "The Natural," Gene Kirby's expertise supported the acting of Robert Redford and co-stars Kim Basinger and Glenn Close.

Gene Kirby, alongside Al Helfer, works a 1951 national college football Game of the Week for Mutual Broadcasting at the Polo Grounds.

KEEPING A LID ON IT

Upon Dizzy Dean's death, widow Pat Dean gave the pitcher-turned-broadcaster's signature Stetson – not to a favorite Cardinals player like Stan Musial, or even to his CBS Game of the Week partner Pee Wee Reese – but to longtime producer and friend Gene Kirby.

The iconic Stetson, perhaps the best-known hat not worn by John Wayne, is now on display at the National Baseball Hall of Fame and Museum in Cooperstown, New York. According to Gene's daughter Sara Kirby Burke, the